YOUTH
HELD
AT THE
BORDER

YOUTH HELD AT THE BORDER

Immigration, Education, and the Politics of Inclusion

LISA (LEIGH) PATEL

FOREWORD BY MICHELLE FINE

Teachers College
Columbia University
New York and London

Published by Teachers College Press, 1234 Amsterdam Avenue, New York, NY 10027

Cataloging-in-Publication data is on file with the Library of Congress.

ISBN 978-0-8077-5389-7 (paperback)
ISBN 978-0-8077-5390-3 (hardcover)

Printed on acid-free paper
Manufactured in the United States of America

19   18   17   16   15   14   13   8   7   6   5   4   3   2   1

This book is dedicated to my mother, Sharda Patel.

Thank you for teaching us how to love, against odds.
Every joy and accomplishment we experience is because of you.

Contents

Dangling Bodies

Stories of Precarity and Courage in Motion

Over coffee, tears, and laughter, I spent a delightful morning stunned at the beauty of Leigh Patel's writing and swept up in the pages of *Youth Held at the Border*, a piercing analysis of how laws move under the skin and penetrate the soul and a tragicomedic musical of young people improvising lives at the dangerous intersection of U.S. immigration, criminalization, education, and welfare policies. On that morning of June 14, 2012, these systems seemed to be finely and punitively aligned, forcing youth into the shadows as they seek to be educated, to be secure, to be loved, and to belong.

And then a day later, on June 15, the *New York Times* tweeted across my cell phone, "Obama to permit young migrants to remain in the U.S.: No deportation for 800,000 who came as children—Congress bypassed." I immediately e-mailed Leigh, who couldn't talk because she was surrounded by "50 crying, very happy DREAMers." I realized then that while many immigrant youth find themselves held at the border by our broken immigration system, these particular youth were *held* by Leigh in an altogether different way. Through her advocacy, these youth are held close and dear on both sides of the border, as she narrates their intimate stories of lives in (e)motion, tracing the track marks of global capital, migrating bodies, and fragile dreams.

In many significant ways, Obama's executive action dramatically alters the life of these 800,000. And yet . . .

The gorgeous young people you are about to meet live lives that, nevertheless, still dangle on the end of highly political pens drafting policies. Their fates are always and profoundly over-determined by the ink of policy makers looking for votes, political action committees (PACs) looking for cheap labor, local police who are forced/invited to enforce federal immigration policy, and educators who want to educate/police our newest Americans. For now they are welcomed into the fabric of the United States, but their stay remains provisional, their security a temporary respite, their inclusion tenuous and precarious. Tomorrow, or by the time you read this text, who knows . . .

Precarity and provisional belonging are seductive American traditions; they circuit through bodies and across time and space promiscuously—native, African American, gay, children with disabilities, poor, immigrant, Muslim. Belonging for these young Americans is always provisional; these young people are asked to be on display and instructed to "stand up straight, make eye contact, wear eyeglasses to appear bright, speak standard English, cut your hair, remove your hijab, go to college, yearn to be upwardly mobile, squeeze yourself into the slim slot for tokens, trust me . . ." And yet they know that they are tacitly being instructed, "Ready yourself to be commodified, objectified, and twisted into a psychic compromise; and always be prepared for quick exit."

A brilliant ethnographer and narrator of lives, Patel handles with grace the intimacies of young people living on the subterranean edge of legality, designing lives of meaning and deep responsibility in the messy ashes of poverty and the shadows of suspect status, with desires to belong in a nation inhabited by immigrants—a nation that nonetheless betrays newcomers when the hue of their skin darkens, politics shift, when we need a new enemy and/or frightened workers desperate enough to hide in the underbelly of an economy built on their backs. Patel is the omniscient narrator, reading the traces of racism, xenophobia, desire, and trauma that litter our national landscape, with seductions of "go to college," "work hard" or "come out of the shadows for 2 years, as long as I am re-elected." Patel insists that readers meet the young women and men who constitute this generation of promises and betrayals. She blows up binaries that circulate with ease, refusing to distinguish undocumented from documented youth, forcing us to bear witness as some of these young people "become undocumented" and then float back into the land of legality, only to return to the liminal space of "maybe legit." Blurring the borders of who belongs, we are invited to travel with bodies in (e)motion.

In this brief and provocative text, we confront a relentless trail of *loss*: intense, material, relational, embodied, collective, and existential loss. Bodies disappear after an ICE raid; a high school culture curdles with the neoliberal intrusion of testing regimes and educational "reforms"; strategic marriages turn bloody, and dreams of college are colonized by debt.

No one would accuse Patel of authoring a romance novel, but she does bathe readers in graceful reflexivity. The text is embroidered with dynamics that haunted Patel's own childhood, questions posed to a brown girl in Nebraska:

"Where are you from?"

Thirty years later she turns to the reader, to confess: "Even at a young age, I couldn't quite fix my mouth to respond to these questions. . . . [H]ow they were being asked and how they deftly positioned me as an outsider and my uninvited interrogator as the insider just felt deeply wrong, and I couldn't begin to put my finger on why." When she is "watching the Patriots play the Bengals" we learn Patel is "football fluent" from her years growing up in the Midwest.

We accompany Patel as she shops for wigs, goes to the movies, barbeques with colleagues, is flooded with memories of her mother sewing and her father self-medicating. We tour the Dominican Republic and the campus of Boston College with her—both analyzed with classic and critical Patel-ian scrutiny.

Patel seasons the text with self-reflexive commentary so that we can see the shared footprints of growing up "other," then and now, as her life braids, over time and space, with these young people fortunate enough to be caressed by her words.

Raised by Sharda Patel, a seamstress with beautiful eyes, a revealing smile, and arms aplenty to hold her babies, a woman who mended torn clothes, Leigh Patel is a generous and gifted storyteller who finds the tears in our national fabric and asks us to stitch ourselves whole. She writes with dual/dueling tongues: to offer insight and incite; to honor and provoke; to reveal existential damage and relentless courage. And so this volume follows the advice of Emily Dickinson, to "tell all the truth, but tell it slant."

A brilliant policy analyst, biting social critic, and loving biographer of lives, Leigh is—despite herself—a stunning romantic smitten with passion for the vitality, humanity, and creativity of these young immigrant lives.

—Michelle Fine

Acknowledgments

This book is the result of many conversations and countless hours spent with immigrant youth and their families in Boston. If they had not allowed me into their homes and lives and encouraged me to tell their stories, this book would not exist. I am also grateful to the dedicated teachers and administrators I knew who worked with these young people. Deep professional rigor and kindness don't always go together, and it was an honor to see this combination exhibited so regularly by these educators.

I also wish to acknowledge Mike Gibbons, an early supporter of this book. A virtual stranger at the time, he insisted that I had to "write a book about these kids!" and checked back in regularly to nudge me along. I am indebted to the tireless and supportive graduate students who acted as background researchers and readers of this work, specifically Rocío Sánchez Ares and Storey Mecoli. There were also many friends and colleagues who read early drafts of chapters and provided invaluable—usually almost immediate!—feedback about what made sense to them and where they wanted to know more: thank you to Janira Arocho, Alex Gurn, Gabriela Fullon, Lara Jirmanus, Bree Picower, and Adiya White-Hammond.

Thank you to my editor, Emily Spangler, for her careful reads, responses, and edits, which immeasurably improved the book and brought it to its final shape. Emily, you helped me to constantly clarify that essential question of writing, "What am I trying to say here?" I also am deeply grateful for the wisdom, support, and writing companionship of Wayne Rhodes. Wayne, our Friday afternoon writing sessions will remain among the most treasured times in my life.

Like all of us, I stand on the shoulders of legends whose work, artistry, and perseverance broke the ground that makes my work possible. I consider essential to my work as a thinker distant scholars like W.E.B. DuBois, Derrick Bell, James Baldwin, Paolo Freire, bell hooks, Zora Neale Hurston, Arundhati Roy, Linda Tuhiwai Smith, and Patricia Hill Collins. I've also had the deep, good fortune to be in close contact with overwhelmingly generous mentors and senior scholars who have helped me shape a hybrid path as public intellectual; thank you, Kathryn Au, María Estela Brisk, Michelle Fine, Kris Gutierrez, and Allan Luke.

Finally, I thank my family, both blood and chosen. You are my heroes and my support system, and I carry you in my heart. Other people might have more words in their acknowledgment, but that's only because it runs so deep with us, it needs fewer.

Preface

On the morning of June 15, 2012, social media outlets exploded with the news that President Obama was going to make an historic announcement about undocumented immigrant youth at 1 P.M. that day. "President to announce relief for DREAMers today at 1. Any watch parties planned?" read one post. Another celebrated: "EPIC win for Dreamers." During the press conference, President Obama summarized a memo from the Secretary of the Department of Homeland Security directing the department to exercise "procedural discretion" (Napolitano, 2012, p. 1) to ascertain on an individual basis if undocumented immigrant youth should be granted 2-year, renewable work permits, contingent upon factors such as successful completion of high school. Just a few days before this announcement, the June 14, 2012, issue of *Time* magazine had featured a dramatic cover of a group of undocumented youth and young adults, with the headline, "We are Americans. Just not legally." It seemed, then, that the stars were aligning for undocumented immigrants to be recognized and valued as worthy members of American society.

As I gathered with dozens of documented and undocumented youth that evening in Dorchester, Massachusetts, the unrelenting theme of the evening was celebration. Bachata, interspersed with reggaeton and compas, provided the pulsing, vibrant soundtrack as immigrant youth, their friends, and allies danced, hugged, cried, and yelled their enthusiasm. Some of the young people were DREAMers, undocumented immigrant youth who had "come out" as undocumented to bring media attention to the DREAM Act and its potential to provide immigrant youth with a pathway to citizenship. As I participated in this celebration, I did so with mixed emotions. I could not help but remember a starkly different scene for immigrant youth not long ago in nearby New Bedford.

On March 6, 2006, the Federal Immigration and Customs Enforcement (ICE) raided the Bianco factory in New Bedford, Massachusetts, sweeping roughly 360 garment workers from the factory—mostly women who worked the first shift of the day—and flew as many as 90 of them that same day to a deportation holding facility in Texas. The raid made national headlines, with most press coverage indicting it as an inhumane sweep of immigrant workers who worked many hours for less than minimum wage at a garment factory that had contracts, ironically, to supply materials to the United States military.

Following ICE's sweep of the factory on March 6, I arrived in New Bedford early that same evening, along with others affiliated in various ways with support services for immigrant populations. I saw lots of fathers and grandmothers giving statements to attorneys. I saw scores of young children being comforted and entertained by the strangers who had come to help. What I did not see were any youth. Anywhere. I went back to New Bedford several times in the following days and weeks, and youth remained elusive. They had, in essence, gone into hiding. Not young enough to need constant care for their physical needs and not yet old enough to be the primary caregivers of their younger siblings, these immigrant youth took cover by disappearing.

The June 2012 celebrations of federal recognition, the young immigrant activists' brave actions of coming out as undocumented in the mainstream press, and the young New Bedford residents' strategy of hiding are all linked as vestiges of how these young people negotiate the politics of inclusion. Immigration, and more so policy and rhetoric about immigration, is in many ways about inclusion—the terms of who is included and on what conditions exclusion is based. As with all politics, particularly those that are premised upon recognition and validation, victories are rarely straightforward and inalienable.

Although the President's introduction to his June 15, 2012, announcement (Office of the Press Secretary, 2012) walked, talked, and sounded like a policy change, it was far from it. He proclaimed that "[undocumented youth] are Americans in their heart, in their minds, in every single way but one: on paper," reading, it would seem, from the same script as the *Time* magazine cover. He then proceeded to outline a change in deportation practices that would, if followed, provide these young people with, at very best, a temporary, imminently revocable, and liminal status in the United States. Moreover, this edict prompts undocumented youth to identify themselves with little to no assurance that their identities will not be used to pursue, detain, and deport them. It also toys with their emotions, gesturing to a sense of morality and investment in humanity but still denying these youth full inclusion in American society. After all, this announcement came from an administration that has shattered previous deportation records, dismally failing to stick to its promise of focusing on "criminal" offenders and showing little hesitation in adding to the profits of the private corrections corporations that indefinitely house detained immigrants. The edict came from an administration trying to get reelected and shed some of its past by flirting with inclusion for an easy-to-love population: undocumented immigrant youth. It will take some time to know the long-term effects and staying power of this announcement, but even from first blush, President Obama's announcement was marked by liminality more than permanency for immigrant youth.

The politics of inclusion are salient to understanding immigrant youth who, neither romanticized as children nor seen as legitimate adults, are particularly vulnerable to quixotic but powerful rhetoric and action affecting immigrant populations. Immigrant youth are severely "underresearched" within academic research and its pockets of migration studies. However, extensive research would not necessarily positively impact their conditions, inasmuch as Western approaches to research have been far from helpful to Indigenous populations (Smith, 1999), as just one grossly understated example. Research that focuses on the ways that immigrant youths are positioned, however, can help us better understand the complexities of who succeeds and who doesn't in society, regardless of the amount of hard work involved. These analyses are crucial to interrupting the inequities that structure society underneath the rhetoric of inclusion, diversity, and opportunity.

Over the past several years, the issue of immigration has regularly splashed across national headlines, dotted picket lines, and swirled in policy circles. Mainstream outrage at "illegal" immigration, particularly since the September 11 attacks, has been bolstered by discourses and slogans about security, safety, and terrorism. The faces of today's wave of immigration to the United States are markedly different from those that characterized previous waves. Unprecedented numbers of migrants from the Global South (especially Asia, Latin America, and the Caribbean) now populate neighborhoods, schools, and workplaces, differing racially and ethnically from previous waves of immigration from European nations. Simultaneously, anti-immigrant, often xenophobic, sentiment among native-born Americans has picked up as well. Over the past years, the numbers and sizes of deportation holding facilities in the United States have grown exponentially, representing an amalgamation of physical construction, law enforcement, and politics that journalist and activist Deepa Fernandes (2007) refers to as the "immigration-industrial complex." Within the public-sector service industry, increasing numbers of immigrants have posed challenges for largely native-born, monolingual, White professionals who don't always understand their clients' needs or how to meet them. In schools, educators and educational policy have focused almost exclusively on increasing the English language fluency of immigrants and children of immigrants. Immigration attorneys have searched for pathways to legal citizenship, sometimes at exorbitant cost to their immigrant clients. Opportunistic business owners have profited from the globally networked economics of low-wage workers moving across national boundaries to find work.

In the midst of these demographic, political, and socioeconomic contexts, young immigrants are also just that: young. I've known the youth in this book across their teenage years and early 20s. By the definitions of developmental psychology, they would be considered adolescents or youths, a stage of life characterized by seeking independence from their parents, striving to find their own identities, and pushing boundaries of adult-led rules. Sociologist Sarah Chinn (2009) documented the ways that adolescence came to signify a time of seeking independence in early-20th-century American culture, when the children of immigrant parents sought to distance themselves culturally from their parents. Chinn profiled immigrants from southern and Eastern Europe who settled in major cities in the northeastern and midwestern United States; it was largely from those populations that the modern concept of adolescence was born. Chin found that it was during this time and cultural space of first-generation youth distancing themselves from their immigrant parents that the concept and terminology truly took hold in the United States. From there, educational psychologists structured a stage of life that has since been synonymous with rebellion and experimentation.

Today's immigrant youth, in circumstances and practices, are both similar to and different from their early-20th-century counterparts. All of the young people you'll meet in these pages perform myriad adult responsibilities. Their family relationships are as complicated as those of any other age group, often more so because of complex family separation and reunification patterns. These young people also sometimes feel squeamish and uneasy in their bodies under the gaze of friends, peers, teachers, and family members. From a societal view, they are in between in many senses: between the stages of child and adult that society is more at ease with; between places where they were born and the nation in which they find themselves; between the warm, temperate weather and family climate of their childhoods and the chilly weather and sometimes even chillier social atmosphere of the northeastern United States. They find themselves caught between a longing for home and a penchant for appropriating the music, patterns, and habits of this new place called Boston that they now inhabit. They live in the interstices, where the strange is becoming familiar and the familiar strange. They, more than any other population I've come to know through my time as a journalist, teacher, and professor, embody the Portuguese word, saudade. Saudade roughly translates to longingness, but also means a remembrance and desire for someone or someplace that doesn't exist anymore or is out of reach. Because of the myriad ways in which home, familiarity, and community are rewritten in the lives of immigrant youth, Western conceptions of adolescence and youth fall abysmally short of speaking to their experiences or providing useful guidance to the professional adults who come into contact with them.

I came to know several undocumented youth in New Bedford following the ICE raid in 2006. One young woman from Guatemala, Ana, still lives in New Bedford. Shortly after the raid and her mother's subsequent deportation, Ana dropped out of high school to work full-time. She and her sister both work as hourly maids for a private cleaning company. They are paid in cash, and in turn, pay for their shelter, food, and clothing in cash. Throughout the years following the immigration raid, they spoke with no native-born adult about their situation, their mother's deportation process, or their own struggles to find and obtain work, shelter, and sustenance. Upon hearing President Obama's 2012 announcement, Ana texted me, saying, "Parece que todavía tengo mi maldición." Ana knew that because she had dropped out of high school, she was not eligible for the President's promissory reprieve; she still was living under her "curse." Ana's story, of working, hiding, hoping momentarily, and being disappointed, is not terribly unique for many immigrant youth, and in its typicality, there is much we can learn about the cracks and fissures in the American dream.

Introduction

If you ask most people what they think of when they hear the word *immigration*, you might hear about legal and illegal crossings, or that this nation was built by immigrants, or perhaps that it is a controversial issue, even a hotbed of political squabbling. Immigration is, in fact, a highly political topic, one that reaches far beyond elected officials to the everyday struggle to be included, in safety, security, and even prosperity. This struggle for inclusion is the bedrock of individual, social, and national identity, one that has always been and continues to be hotly debated. Seemingly straightforward, being included in any social context brings to the surface the implicit and explicit laws of inclusion, as well as who guards those boundaries. In other words, it is at the heart of deeming who is worthy and who is not.

Newcomer immigrant youth fully embody this struggle and offer a unique perspective on the laws of inclusion and exclusion in America. In this book I tell their stories to analyze not just how immigrant youth experience the United States but the core ways in which national, economic, social, and political borders are drawn and redrawn. Instead of the ideal of the land of opportunity, immigrant youth often encounter myriad new borders, long after the physical migration from one country to another is over. To understand the politics of inclusion, we must explore their largely unknown and often unspoken experiences of aspirations and denial. We also must push past the easy appearances of inclusion when they merely serve to maintain an inequitable, problematic social order. In other words, we must resist facile comfort that because different populations might be included in some aspects of a society, therefore meaningful, comprehensive, and just inclusion in society's structures is happening.

Sociologists (e.g., Bourdieu, 1990) use the metaphor of structure to explain that people's actions should be viewed in relation to ways of acting, thinking, and being that are shaped by society. Societal structure can be understood as similar to the human body's skeletal structure. Across individuals, the skeleton includes mostly the same components that govern the systemic biological processes such as breathing and eating. From one person to the next, though, these processes can vary greatly, often due not just to the individual's unique characteristics but also to external factors.

1

The documentary series *Unnatural Causes* (California Newsreel, 2008) focuses on the ways in which individuals' health is significantly impacted by their external environments, and those impacts reflect societal differences of privilege and oppression. The episode "When the Bough Breaks" investigates the disproportionately high incidences of infant mortality and low birth weight of children born to African American mothers. In contrast to native-born White American mothers, babies from African American mothers are four times more likely to be premature and three times more likely to die before their first birthday. These statistics are alarming. What could be the cause? The documentary discusses and dismisses the following factors: genetics, socioeconomic level, country of origin, and even level of education. African American women with college degrees have worse infant mortality rates than White women with only a high school degree.

The documentary focuses on one successful African American lawyer and the medical complications suffered by her daughter, who was born prematurely and with a birth weight low enough to relegate her to a neonatal unit for the first month of her life. She describes her situation: "I did all the right things. I ate well, I rested, I took prenatal vitamins, and saw my doctor. And still, there I was with my premature baby in the hospital with all these tubes coming out of her."

After eliminating the more traditional explanations for health disparity like individual personal habits, the only remaining possibility was to look for what African American women—and not African or White American women—had in common, and that was the stress of living in a discriminatory society. Over time, human systems that encounter high stress levels from the daily microaggressions of discrimination manifest this stress biophysically. One researcher likened the accumulation of these daily stresses to constantly revving a car engine; the integrity of the engine will begin to show signs of undue wear and tear. African American women experience more everyday racism in the contact zone of society than White or African women do, and this has a deleterious effect on infant mortality rates. This case and the surrounding research behind it highlight the ways in which—while we are independent, thoughtful beings—we all nevertheless live within structures in society, and those structures bring to bear more harmful effects on some of us than on others. Similarly, we can understand societal components such as work, education, and family in relation to what people do, who they come into contact with, and how they think. As with the body, the ways that human beings interact within those structures is influenced by the structure and, in turn, influences the structure. In this book the structures of age, gender, race, and culture will be discussed, with particular and consistent attention paid to the institution of schooling.

Schooling has long been one of the most pervasive institutions for reflecting and shaping individuals' relationships to society (e.g., Lareau, 2011). In schools, implicit rules often start delineating from very young ages who is included and who is excluded from particular forms of participation. For example, in her landmark study Barrie Thorne (1993) detailed the ways in which gender socialization occurs in explicit and pervasive ways in schooling, shaping what it means to be a socially accepted boy and girl. For immigrants, as with native-born youths, school is also one of the places to meet other kids, build a daily routine, and, with any luck, have a mentor or caring adult who notices when you don't show up. I came to know most, but not all, of the youths in this book through my professional collaboration with an all-immigrant high school in Boston. A public school with the specific mission of serving recently immigrated youth, Franklin High School (all identifying names of places and people have been changed to protect identities) was small, with only about 200 students. Located in a central part of the city, the school's population at the time that I knew it was roughly 50% Dominican, 20% Cape Verdean, 10% Central American (Guatemala and El Salvador), 10% Haitian, and 10% from Southeast Asia and Eastern Europe. The school therefore simultaneously boasted and struggled with many different first languages, varied prior experiences with education, and various premigration interactions with the United States.

Franklin High School followed an international model of schooling, which meant it served only recently immigrated youth from countries all around the world. Across the country, there are over a dozen official international schools (Internationals Network for Public Schools, 2011) in public school systems. Generally speaking, because international schools work exclusively with newcomer immigrant youth, they prioritize explicit support of English language learning along with the state-defined curriculum. In many ways, Franklin High School was unique because of this focus, but in many other ways, it was like every other public high school. Resources were tight, new teachers often didn't know the issues facing lesser advantaged populations in public schools, and the promise of education as the great equalizer in a stratified society was dubious at best. Even in a school in which there was an explicit commitment to supporting the acquisition of a new language for all, who benefitted the most was not always a simple matter of effort and merit. In other words, Franklin High was like every other school in that it sometimes interrupted and sometimes reflected uneven opportunities for inclusion in society.

I spent 6 years in close contact with this school. I worked with its teachers on how to teach academic language and with its students on both academic and nonschool issues and problems. With staff members, I developed an after-school homework support program that introduced many of the students to their first college campus and, in my last years in the school, I ran an internship project that combined professional internships with critical education about society. I worked with youth as coresearchers, acted as advocates for them in immigration hearings, and conducted dozens upon dozens of interviews with them and their closest friends and family members. Throughout my one-on-one work with youth and the support that I provided in their classrooms, I came to feel like and be treated as an ad hoc member of the school staff, with the enviable position of being able to know the school and how it was perceived by insiders and outsiders.

Franklin High, in most of the years that I was lucky enough to be part of that community, was a special place. For example, it is not uncommon for former students to go back and visit their high schools, but in most high schools, it is the kids who were the stars, who were student council representatives, prized athletes, or National Honor Society members who come back to visit what was a place of laudation for them. At Franklin High, this practice did not follow the pattern of favorite, smartest, or most likely to _____ (fill in the blank). Not all the students came back to visit, but most did, and that included even the kids for whom studying is like watching paint dry, because for many of the students and adults, the school was not just a place of academics but also personal connection. It was a special place, and what made it special was its size, its staff, its students, and its mission, to differing degrees depending on whom you ask and when you ask them.

The school had a reputation among the students and their families as a community, a place where people from different cultures and nations were united by their commonalities, where students had to worry less about their lack of English fluency or their accent than they might in other schools. When I asked Rebecca, a young Dominican woman, what she found to be different in this school compared to the more typical American middle school she had attended, she told me: "There's too many things that are so different. My other school was like crazy, and this one is much better. And here, everybody is like me cuz they are from another country. So nobody makes fun of me for having an accent. I talk more here, so my English gets better here." For Rebecca, the school offered a place where she was more easily included. Dozens of students, from various linguistic and cultural backgrounds, told me the same thing that Rebecca had, that they felt a sense of family at Franklin, even resembling the ways that family will love and tease at the same time.

As with any school, though, there were seamier sides than appeared readily on the surface but which often reflected the larger social contexts surrounding the school. For example, despite the focus on tolerance and diversity, racial tensions emerged. For many years, the school was numerically and culturally dominated by students from the Dominican Republic, and Spanish was the lingua franca of the hallways and gathering places. These facts along with decades-old trajectories of racial tension, contributed to the perception that the school was not as friendly a place for Haitian students as it was for Spanish speaking, especially Dominican, students. In just this way, Franklin High School and the experiences of its youth mirror back the ways in which schooling and the nation have a complicated set of relationships between oft-invoked discourses about multiculturalism, diversity, and the lived realities of racism and discrimination. In this instance, inclusion was mediated by racialized identities, with influences from both American and Caribbean legacies of segregation and persecution. In keeping with this nation's collective consciousness, the youth at Franklin experienced both opportunities to be included for their accents or language challenges, and then in another moment, exclusion for their racial backgrounds. The school, like other schools and like the nation itself, was a mix of complicated and often contradictory messages.

The Franklin High School depicted in this book no longer exists. Although the building is still there, and the school continues to operate, like everyone and everything else, it has changed. The demographics of the school have shifted so that there is not one dominant national background in the school. There are even more countries represented in the student body makeup. And there have been significant changes in staff, faculty, and the culture of the school. The school in these pages should stand on its own for its unique features and also be read as emblematic of patterns of opportunities lost and seized in every high school.

How to Read and Misread Franklin High School

I write this in a time when a teaching profession mostly made up of White, native-born, monolingual teachers is faced with growing numbers of immigrant students; as many as 1 in 5 school children come from an immigrant home in which English is not the primary language. Particularly in this context, my analysis of an all-immigrant high school could be misread as a model for how pedagogy should happen for all English language learners or ELLs, as immigrant pupils are known in education parlance. Education, like most applied fields of practice, is very fond of models and examples of "best practices." However, one of the reasons why schools are such a robust way to understand society is that they are unrelentingly fraught with dynamics of ability, race, class, and gender. As such, taking what has been seen to "work" in one context and using it another context is an underestimation of the power of social contexts and the deeply dynamic nature of human beings. It is a mistake that we seem to frequently make in applied fields like education. Franklin High School, like all high schools, was a three-dimensional entity where adults and youth came together in wonderful and flawed ways. Borne of an understandable desire to address social problems at large scales, when we look at Franklin, or any other school, as a model, we tend to gloss over the not-so-ideal realities and fix our attention on what "works." In that focus, we quickly obscure the fact that what "works" is always being defined implicitly and explicitly for a particular goal, by particular people, and often benefits some more than others. In a yearning for a model, then, we must be diligent about not overlooking the core lessons that can be learned in the dynamics of that context and then be cautious in comparison to other contexts.

Legal or Not

In some classes, as many as half of Franklin's high school students were undocumented, meaning that they did not have legal immigration status in the United States. Even though the venerable *New York Times* and many of the kids and their families used the terminology *being illegal*, I do not. I sympathize with media campaigns that hold that "No human being is illegal," (Sen, 2003), which point out the inconsistent ways in which poor populations of color are called illegal but other, more advantaged populations, such as businesspeople are said to have committed illegal acts but are rarely, if ever, referred to wholesale as illegal people. My linguistic choice, though, is motivated by a different concern. When we call one person *illegal*, that implies that everyone else, those who have experienced better luck in their circumstances, is *legal*. With this one simple word, we depict a reality in which individuals are autonomous, omnipotent, and agentic, and we invoke an image of a legal system that is simply acknowledging individuals who "play" according to the rules. Using the reductive dichotomy of *legal* and *illegal* obscures the complexity of the political, economic, and cultural factors that permeate the push and pull of human capital across borders. As I listened to the stories of these youth, spent time with their families, and worked with their teachers and principals, I learned about the forces that had shaped their stories of migration, the newly found borders within the United States, and how they made sense of their aspirations in these contexts. None of these complex and very personal stories can be understood through the lens of one person being a legal immigrant and another not. In fact, this is one of the key focal points of the book: to situate the narratives and lives of immigrant youth within a societal context, in which immigration is less the result of individual choice than of global forces of politics and economics.

A Word About Research and Perspective

It is not without hesitation that I asked these young people for permission to tell their stories, especially since many of them will not benefit directly from the publication of this book and their stories are not easy ones to tell, with happy endings, let alone beginnings and middles. Additionally, there has long been a disturbing trend on the part of more advantaged researchers to describe vulnerable populations, such as recently immigrated youth, and in so doing, ascribe this or that set of characteristics to these groups (Wolfe, 1991). This tendency to pinpoint the characteristics of a group as if they are static is both impossible and often more serving to an observer's gaze (Morrow & Richards, 1996). However, as I traversed the worlds they live in and the worlds occupied by most adults who come into contact with them, such as teachers and social workers, it became more and more obvious that these stories hold significant lessons about immigrants, about America, about the ideals by which it defines itself, and the ways in which it actually opens doors unevenly. The stories of immigrant youth may assist you in knowing better what it feels like to be excluded in myriad ways. In this sense, the book itself may act as a contact zone (Pratt, 1991), bringing together the knowledge you have of the world through your daily practices, with the pathways, practices, and realities faced by some immigrant youths.

Whether or not the stories of these youth hold new insights for you personally, they illuminate how the conditions of inclusion are named, maintained, and protected, and by whom. As Melissa Harris-Perry (2011) put it in her work on Black women, "it is important to understand political processes through the vulnerable human lives that are part of the larger story."

For many of the youth in this book, telling their stories involves a personal risk of deportation with which they did not feel comfortable. Other undocumented youth have chosen to "come out" as undocumented as a way of explicitly defying what are often spun to be cruel deportation policies. Similarly, these youth told their stories to me and agreed to being portrayed here, with their identities protected through pseudonyms, as a way of arguing back against the sequestering they experienced as immigrants, as racially minoritized, as undocumented, as criminal. Their stories demand to be told, as part of the ability to vilify populations rests upon people being seen in simplistic, two-dimensional characterizations, here of undocumented youth as illegal, criminal, and incapable victims. In telling these stories, I affirm that the youth who are profiled in this book are as wonderful, problematic, and varied as any other group of human beings.

As I share their stories here and provide analysis, my perspective is influenced by my own experience first and foremost as the daughter of immigrants. I was raised by a mother who did not attend school beyond the elementary years in her rural village in India and then managed to support her small nuclear family by hemming the pants and skirts of strangers. I also write as a daughter who soaked up intended and unintended lessons from an embittered, usually unemployed, and alcoholic father whose internalized racism taught him that to be anything but a successful White American was to be lesser. These lessons included understanding how status and capital, including racialized identity, permeates life in the United States.

An upbringing by parents who support their family through physical labor and characterized by some amount of *cultural cringe* is familiar territory to low-income immigrant youth of color. It is part of what has allowed me to connect well with dozens of young immigrants and their families, understanding, for example, why a Cape Verdean grandmother bristled to hear her granddaughter speaking Spanish more fluently than English. I understood, too, why the granddaughter rebelled against her grandmother's wish that she speak Cape Verdean Creole, which felt restrictive despite her own ambivalence about her emerging comfort in Spanish and decreasing fluency in her native language. The daughter of immigrants, I, too, am more fluent in languages other than my parents'. I have both experienced personally and studied academically these types of cultural disjunctions. Simply put, my own cultural background is, like all writers, part of what compels me to tell these stories and contributes another layer of perspective to my analysis of them.

I also tell their stories through the lens of a sociologist, analyzing these individual stories for information about the world we live in and the opportunities and restrictions inherent in our respective places in that world. Lastly, I tell their stories as an educator, a former high school teacher who still acts as the teacher, mentor, tutor, and sometimes disciplinarian of youth, including the immigrant youth found in these pages who have been in my life for years. I've known them as they've struggled through high-stakes assessments in school, navigated police states in their homelands and neighborhoods, worked long hours to support family members here and at home, and tried to understand why working hard and being a good person doesn't always translate into being fully included in society. Or to put it more aptly, why it works out for some and not others. As Davey, a young immigrant from Cameroon, looked around the elite private university campus where I taught and saw scores of undergraduates wearing designer clothing, talking on the latest and smartest phones on the market, and spending on a coffee what he might pay for a meal, he asked, "Why they got it so good? They only speak one language and only know one place, right? We all [immigrant youth] have to know three or four. Or five. Can you explain that to me?" Well, this book is my best shot, Davey. Over the course of this book I will offer an analysis and explanation of how immigrant youth are positioned in U.S. society. My explanation is meant not as a justification for the gap in opportunities to be included in the American dream of success but rather an analysis that speaks to Davey's highly cogent observation and question. Without such analyses, any conversation about inclusion and participation in society is likely to rest upon shallow rhetoric. To know what to do about the nation's immigration problem, or how to best serve our most vulnerable populations, we need to know the details of these lives and the social conditions that make them so.

This book is narrative-led, meaning that the sociological analysis is anchored in the stories and details of immigrant youth. Each chapter opens with an ethnographic description followed by analysis of its context. Chapters 1–7 of the book provide narratives and analyses clustered around, respectively, the high school and postsecondary years. While these sections are grounded in the context of school and education, there are many societal factors that intersect with education. Throughout these chapters, using both narratives and analysis, I demonstrate the ways in which gender, age, life-stage expectations, work responsibilities, documentation status, and racialization all intersect to shape life opportunities for immigrant youth. I draw attention to the isolating effect of these factors, relegating youth to circumscribed zones of living, with little substantive contact outside of low-income immigrant diaspora contexts. Chapters 8–12 of the book situate immigrant youth's experiences within broader globalized contexts that push and pull people to migrate across nation-state borders. In this section, I carry through the realities of life as an immigrant youth to illuminate that ways in which both privileged and marginalized youth are positioned in societal zones and where there are opportunities for interrupting these patterns in everyday interactions.

This book is not a book solely about education, but it is situated in schooling inasmuch as schools reflect much of what is good and problematic about society, particularly for young people. It is not a work of history or law, but it relies on the history of immigration and immigration law as a frame for understanding contemporary politics of inclusion and exclusion. It is not a biography, but it gives some youths an opportunity to tell their stories. It is not a traditional social science text, but it makes use of empirical data. Across the whole volume, the work of the book, and of the reader, is the same: to know better the ways in which pathways are constructed in society and where there are opportunities for altering these pathways for a more equitable society, one that might begin to embody principled inclusion rather than reactionary exclusion.

CHAPTER ONE

Wana: Wigs, Husbands, and Documentation

As a community-based youth researcher, I often find myself in schools, churches, workplaces, and colleges. About the last place discussed in guidebooks as a site for research is a wig shop. There I was, though, wig shopping with Wana, a young Haitian woman I had known for 5 years. Wana immigrated to the United States from her home of Port-au-Prince in Haiti in 2005. Since that time, she had learned social and academic English fluently, graduated from high school, worked to support herself and her family back in Haiti, and doggedly pursued higher education in the hope of becoming a nurse. During this time Wana also navigated an uneasy and often murky field of documentation status, working with advocates and trying to avoid charlatans but not always succeeding in telling the difference between the two.

Our wig shopping date stemmed from a case of mistaken identity. I had arranged to meet Wana at a downtown subway stop. Scanning the crowds, it took me several minutes to spot Wana's familiar face across the stop waiting area, under her new blonde bob-cut wig. Her small frame was shaking with laughter.

"I couldn't find you! Look at you!" I exclaimed, stating the obvious and laughing myself.

"I know, I could see you looking; it's funny," Wana said, between more laughs.

"What is this? I didn't even know you had wigs; I've never seen you in one."

"Oh yes, you know, Miss, we can't always look the same day after day, and I like this one. What do you think?" she asked, smoothing stray hairs that weren't stray at all.

"It's fantastic; you look like a different version of you. J'aime bien cette fille donc je souviens (I like this young woman who I remember)." "Oui, oui, je suis la meme fille (Oh yes, I'm the same girl); Miss, you should get one, too. I'll take you. I can show you." And so we decided that I should be initiated into the world of wigs, and Wana should be my guide.

On that day, Wana was wearing a very typical outfit for her: snug white jeans and layered cotton shirts in teal and white that also fit her to a T. The color of her shoes matched the teal hue of one of the shirts exactly. This coordination was not an accident, nor was it the result of expensive shopping trips. Wana, like most working-class, young, female immigrants, earned very little money for many hours of work in a service industry (Hondagneu-Sotelo, 2007). Wana worked as a nurse's aid in an assisted living facility, where she ran errands for patients, checked on them, and maintained their rooms and bathrooms. For this work, which she was quite happy to have, she earned $8.50/hour. She worked approximately 30 hours a week while she attended high school, and increased those hours when she graduated. Her earnings amounted to a biweekly check for roughly $350. She always did three things with these checks: She put aside $80 in her savings; she gave her aunt and uncle, with whom she lived, about $150; and she visited a Moneygram location to send $50 to her mother and sisters living in Port-au-Prince. Moneygram, like other money transfer companies, charge baseline fees of $10 per transaction. If you're sending large amounts of money, their fees are reasonable, as the fee remains around that $10 mark even in much larger amounts into the thousands. However, most of Moneygram's clients are not sending thousands of dollars; the majority of Moneygram's business comes from globalized, or transnational, families of migrants, living across political nation/state borders as well as geographic oceans and sending monetary remittances to countries of origin. In fact, since the mid-1990s, the number of companies like Moneygram has increased while the fees they charge have fallen. The market has grown and become more competitive as migration has grown, particularly from the Global South to the north. It is estimated that remittances to Haiti alone amount to more than a billion dollars per year, and this is just a portion of the monetary flow to countries in Latin America and the Caribbean (Orozco, 2006). Haiti's economy depends on an estimated $1.5 billion in remittances from Haitians living in the United States (Rindenbro, 2011). Money is largely sent through banks, informal couriers, and transfer companies. Even with fee reductions that were provided temporarily by Moneygram and Western Union, the largest U.S.-based wire companies, immigrants like Wana typically lose 15–20% of often extremely hard-earned money to fees. This kind of structured economic challenge is part of what makes it difficult for immigrants, already low-income, to become upwardly mobile. There is not much to save or dispose of outside of family obligations and the significant cost of simply being low-income. A basic fact of life in the United States and many other nations is that it costs more money to be poor (Schiller, 2007). For immigrant youth, who do not typically receive the scaffolded economic socialization that is more commonplace for wealthier, native-born youth, such as bank accounts opened with weekly allowances, these costs compound, vie for their attention with schooling, and often win.

After the remittance for her mother, Wana used the remaining money, which usually amounted to $30 per week, to buy food and clothing for herself and, whenever possible, save every other penny. When she did buy clothes, she almost always frequented the Haitian shops along Blue Hill Avenue in Dorchester or Mattapan that featured the whites and bright colors of the tropical isles. Blues, greens, and yellows dominated Wana's clothes and jewelry. Even in the winter months, underneath her faux black leather coat, the hues of Wana's long sleeves and sweaters communicated her tropical origins far from the blustery winters of Boston.

Her outfits also reflected the particular persona and something of the history of this highly industrious and thoughtful young woman who paid deliberate attention to details. As she recalled:

> You know who taught me how to always look good and be nice to everyone? My father. I worked with him in his restaurant, and he always show me how to look good, professional, to be nice to everyone, but not too nice, you know? You have to not show favorites, you have to be able to be ready for any person you are going to meet, the person who lends the restaurant money at the bank, and the person who takes the garbage away, for everybody.

Even though Wana's father had abandoned her and her siblings when she was still young, she had been deeply influenced by his words and example. Wana could have been the poster child for the saying that you should dress for the job that you want and she could add a few pointers on how to behave yourself around others you mean to impress, even if you don't immediately see a possibility for how they might affect your future. She was, without fail, mature, confident, collected, and pleasant. According to one of her favorite teachers, her confidence sometimes even surpassed a realistic appraisal of the situation in front of her. And she has been that way since I've known her, throughout most of her teen years and into her 20s. Her confidence in guiding me through the wig shop was genuine, and she enjoyed it immensely.

What Wana does not project, quite intentionally, is how she has struggled personally in navigating her documentation status in the United States. When her stepmother, a U.S. citizen, was permanently separated from Wana's father, it blocked Wana's most direct route to a green card under United States immigration law. However, it took Wana some time to accept this reality and adjust her strategies to secure citizenship in response. For close to a year after the separation, she communicated with her stepmother, a U.S. citizen, and made trips to visit her in Miami in order to convince her to sponsor Wana's application for residency. She appealed unsuccessfully to her stepmother's sense of family ties, to female solidarity, to her sense of empathy.

As Wana's time on a legal work visa drew to a close, she became undocumented, meaning that the many daily interactions that involve filling out a piece of paper had now become risky and undesired. Wana learned how to avoid situations like applying for a new job that would demand documentation that she did not have, forcing her to make choices like staying in a job that didn't provide flexible hours for a student. Although she had always been financially responsible, Wana's undocumented status forced her to take special care to maintain a spotless record with her phone company and bank, her two sources of financial history in the United States. Because any new paperwork involved risk, maintaining existing networks and their illusion of safety was vital.

All undocumented people learn to maintain invisibility at all costs. They do this by maintaining rapid and narrow circuits of travel between home, school, and sometimes work. They stay in vulnerable housing and work contexts both because it's what they can afford and because being around other immigrants feels less risky and less visible than standing out in another community. With any kind of visibility comes the risk of deportation. If deported, the ramifications would come not only to the immigrant but also to the family. In Wana's very typical case, deportation would mean that she would no longer be able to help support her family. She would also be navigating a much more violent and volatile life, and she would most certainly not be able to pursue a professional career in health care.

Over the course of the next year or so, she began to see herself more and more as "illegal," both in terms of the daily details of navigating this exclusionary identity and her self-image. This shadowed her desire and drive to succeed. Without a doubt, her motivation took a nosedive when she had to loosen her grip on going to college and becoming a nurse. As an undocumented student, Wana could not access federal financial aid and in Massachusetts, like 38 other states in the union, even if undocumented immigrant youth have graduated from U.S. high schools and gained admittance to college, they must pay international student rates, often three to four times the rate of in-state tuition. As she faced these purposeful obstacles to higher education, for a short time, Wana's grades in high school suffered, she began to feel lethargic, and she didn't like herself very much. She struggled to make sense of what wrong she had done that warranted such a bottleneck of opportunity, and she often, like many undocumented youth, came up short of an explanation that would reconcile her own failure to fit into the ideal that people of good character and ambition deserved to succeed. In short, she became depressed.

Meritocracy, the idea that one's destiny and path is largely determined by one's actions, is a common explanation for success. *You deserved it! You worked so hard! Couldn't happen to a better person!* And when we are told these things, we all enjoy the laudatory vibe, sometimes demurring with humility but rarely offering a different explanation other than hard work and sometimes luck. However, the flip side of meritocracy also implies, with grueling efficiency, that individuals don't succeed because they haven't deserved it, worked hard enough for it, or just aren't good people. Without ever being uttered aloud, these values are the ones that shape the self-concept of immigrants like Wana who struggle to understand why seemingly relentless obstacles dominate their lives. Particularly for young immigrants, whose pathways are stitched into the fabric of their families' hopes and aspirations, not securing financial and personal security is tantamount to collective failure of the family. In Wana's mind, she saw herself as unworthy because she could not be a successful nurse as she had planned when she immigrated to the United States. She felt shame not just for herself but also for her family.

In addition to the feelings of failure and inadequacy experienced by young immigrants when they cannot access college, get a driver's license, or obtain fairly paid work, they also experience social isolation as a result of being undocumented. Their opportunities to build social networks that might provide opportunities to make personal and professional connections, improve communication skills, and become involved with community are limited by their undocumented status. The mental health profession struggles to effectively reach women from minority ethnic backgrounds, not to mention those who are undocumented (Latta & Goodman, 2005). Being undocumented presents a potentially damaging mix of social isolation, self-doubt, and, frequently, poverty, that is only beginning to be understood by social services in America. Left to their own capacities and often isolated, undocumented immigrants live out daily existences within limited circles close to home and work.

With the road to residency seemingly closed off to Wana, she faced the options of staying in the United States without legal documentation while continuing to work and study slowly or returning to Haiti and starting her life over there, without any financial base and amidst the upheaval that has marked the capital city, her home, since the U.S.-backed removal of Haitian President Jean Bertrand Aristide from office. Neither option was terribly compelling, but Wana's steadfast aspiration to be a nurse kept her in the United States, where she worked and took whatever classes she could afford after her rent, utilities, and remittances back home were paid. Because she no longer had authorized documentation status, she had to register as an international student at her community college and pay over $1,000 for a single class. She maintained a heavy pace of work and part-time study and socialized exclusively through her church, a Baptist church in a suburb south of Boston. It was in church that she met Morgan, a native Bostonian who would court Wana, marry her, and subsequently control, harass, and abuse her until she divorced him.

Thinking back later to Wana's laughing face and joyful confidence at the wig shop, it was no mystery to me why Morgan would be attracted to Wana. Added to the physical attractiveness of her small and fit frame, her tidy hair, and her bright eyes was Wana's charm and a quick wit, even in her third language of English. But the first time I met Morgan, at a showing of *Aristide,* a documentary about the former Haitian president shown at MIT as part of their Pan-African film series, it wasn't precisely love that was in the air. The

small theater was filled with younger and older activists, most African American, some Haitian American, and the room was sprinkled with conversations
in English, Haitian Creole, and French. Wana had told me she was bringing a
friend, and she watched my face intently as she introduced me to Morgan, in
his khaki pleated pants and striped polo shirt.

"Oh, hi, how do you, uh, know Wana?" I glanced at Wana, but her face
revealed very little.

"From church." Looking around, holding two paper plates, one with chips
and one with pizza. "What is this? An MIT thing?"

"Yeah, it's part of a film series [I feared Pan-African might be over the top
for this initial exchange] they do here, but there are a lot of people from other
places in the city. Um, what do you do, Morgan?" Try as I might, I could not
quite take the interrogatory tone out of my voice as I searched for information
from this forty-something American-born White man who was accompanying
my young friend and looking everywhere but at Wana or me.

"I'm a teacher."

"Miss Patel is a professor at Boston College," Wana interjected. "I already
told him about you and how I am helping you with your work."

"Um, yeah, that's right. I work with immigrant youth in the city, and I've
known Wana here for about 3 years now."

Morgan took this in. Or not. "What do you teach at BC?"

"I teach courses on literacy and on research."

Morgan makes a connection here, "Oh, I have to take some kind of reading
course for my certification. Think you can help me with that?" he asks, smiling
slyly to make it clear that by help he doesn't mean amplify his comprehension
but rather curtail his work.

"No." In that moment, my read of Morgan taking advantage of Wana over-
rode any inclination I might have had as a literacy educator to assist this man.

When the film showing was over, Wana and I caught a few minutes to
speak privately. As she explained it, Morgan wanted to help her and even had
some idea of her situation concerning documentation status. I told her that
it was clear and understandable to me that documentation status was uniting
the two, but I also voiced my concern for her safety. I wanted to know more.
What did she know about this guy? How long had she known him? She assured me that she would be careful, but this was cold comfort to me and,
perhaps, to her also.

Wana had previously resisted the suggestions of many in her extended
family that she find an American to marry. They suggested Price, a United
States citizen who managed a restaurant in Miami, and also Jimmy, a much older man whom Wana had met and had not liked very much. Within immigrant
communities, talk of potential marriage allies and marriage brokers abounds. *I
got a cousin who is perfect, lives in New York. Oh, remember that girl from the party, she liked
you. She has her green card, you know? Her auntie wants to get her married, too.*

"I don't want to marry for that. I want to be with someone because of love, you know?" she had explained. Even a cursory understanding of migration law and restrictions, though, suggests how this association between love and marriage can be compromised when an unauthorized documentation status holds a grip on every facet of life.

Perhaps it was the cognitive, emotional, and financial wear and tear of being undocumented that changed Wana's mind about marrying a native-born American for documentation. With all other pathways to citizenship blocked from her, this was one of the few options Wana had outside of living in constant fear of deportation, which she had been doing for a few years by the time she met Morgan.

So she decided to marry Morgan. When I raised questions again about why she had chosen Morgan and not some of the other "suitors" her family had suggested, she said that she understood Morgan, could deal with him. In other words, she thought she was smarter than Morgan and could remain in control of the situation.

They were married in a small ceremony at his grandfather's house where her aunt and uncle attended, alongside the 20 people from Morgan's extended family, longtime residents of his small town about 40 miles south of Boston. Wana moved into Morgan's one-bedroom apartment in the same town, a town that has a somewhat dualistic population comprised of mostly working-class, longtime residents descended from Irish and Italian immigrants and a quickly growing Haitian and Dominican population. These populations don't mix often, and when they do, they don't mix easily. At the counter of a Haitian restaurant in the town, a sign reads, "Proud to be American-owned and English-operated," a concession designed to speak to nativist reactions to changing demographics and ingratiate the restaurant to the larger White community. Despite the town's not-so-distant history as an immigrant community, its memory of its origins is selective among inhabitants who feel secure in their identity as American and suddenly feel that place threatened by the new wave of immigrants. Towns like Morgan's and even entire states have reacted against immigration in the form of restrictive laws. For example, Prince William County in Virginia, a suburb of Washington, D.C., passed one of the first anti-immigrant laws in 2007, requiring police officers to check the documentation status of any detainee. Similar legislation has been passed in Arizona, Georgia, and Alabama. Prince William County experienced significant fallout from this legislation, including mass migration of residents, business and home foreclosures, decreased school enrollment, and public relations problems, events interpreted by some as cautionary tales (Bahrampour, 2010).

When Wana moved in with Morgan, she brought all of her belongings with her: her clothes, her photo albums, and a few used books she had bought when she was initially learning English. She used her money to buy other items for the apartment, a painting here, a decorative bowl there, going through about $250 of her savings. Morgan suggested that in addition to creating a home together, they should have joint bank accounts, arguing that this would look better for her residency application. Wana agreed to this and some other big changes, like quitting one of her two part-time jobs. Because her new home necessitated a two-hour commute to work on public transportation each way, and because she was living rent-free with Morgan, her expenses were lower. Morgan also reminded her that with her marriage license and soon-to-be-submitted green card application, she could register for college classes at cheaper in-state tuition rates. Morgan, like everyone else, knew that college was paramount for Wana and made his case for merging their assets stronger by appealing to her priorities and her dreams of a green card and college. Although she had a concrete pathway to citizenship, Wana, after she married Morgan, was in many ways even less included in work and study that would offer her opportunities for social advancement. Her significant time commuting between the city and this suburb also meant that she was not spending those hours talking with classmates or professors. While on paper Wana would seem to have more secure access to inclusion in American society, the daily realities were that she was much more isolated, not just geographically but socially and professionally. These are the ways that social conditions shape the opportunities and restrictions that amount to advancement and stasis in society.

When Wana speaks now of Morgan, she blames herself for agreeing to marry him, for moving away from her family and the neighborhood she came to know, for depositing her paychecks into their joint account, for everything. But she can also recall the increasingly aggressive actions that Morgan took that now make her regret her choices. It began with Morgan surveying her cell phone to see whom she was calling and texting: "I got mad at him, you know? I don't give him any reason to be watching me like that, looking at my things. And, anyway, I don't like him to look at my things. Nobody do that." Well, Morgan did. Morgan also made it clear whenever he didn't approve of her actions. On the one occasion that I visited Wana in the apartment she shared with Morgan, she prepared a beautiful dinner of roasted chicken, salad, and potatoes. We ate at the kitchen table while Morgan sulked in front of the TV, watching the Patriots play the Bengals. Having spent most of my teen years in Nebraska, I am football fluent, so I watched a few plays and made a few comments about shotgun passes and zone defense. These went nowhere, with Morgan muttering "yeah" and not taking his eyes away from the set. When I took my cue to go back into the kitchen, Wana laughed this off, whispering to me, "He gets like that sometimes. But then he's OK. I just wait until he is OK." Her rationalization was familiar to me; I had lived this cycle and sometimes conversation with my mother and siblings on many an occasion, listening to her tell us to keep it quiet and stay in our rooms until our father calmed down. Semi-literate in

English, with three young children, and raised in a culture where her duty in life was to be a good (read: obedient) wife and mother, what else could she do? Coming from this history, though, to me it was obvious that Morgan's power plays of sulking and pouting, on top of the large power differential inherent in their respective residency statuses, were reason to be concerned about the relationship. Wana, on the other hand, did not see Morgan's mood swings as anything to be concerned with. Having never lived with a mercurial person, she had not developed the hypervigilance that comes with knowing that the sulk might escalate into something else.

On the February morning when Morgan's sulking did escalate into grabbing, pushing, and shaking her because she "wasn't doing what [he] told her," as she later related, Wana made a quick exit into the bedroom. She locked the door, called her aunt and waited for her uncle to get off work and come get her. Morgan alternately pounded on the door and apologized, saying that he was just angry and she knew he didn't mean it. In the days and weeks that followed, Morgan followed Wana to work and was often sitting in his car waiting for her when she left the building. She came to rely on her uncle and other family members to give her rides to and from work and school. Now, in addition to fearing immigration officials, she was also forced to fear Morgan. Although she knew that Morgan's treatment of her was wrong, she did not report his actions out of fear of deportation. On top of the shame and guilt that abused women often feel, Wana's situation echoes the plight of many immigrant women who become trapped in similar domestic abuse situations. Studies estimate that 59.5% of immigrant married women experience abuse as compared to 48.6% of married U.S.-born women, and these are conservative estimates because approximating rates of any type of contexts for both domestic abuse and unauthorized immigrants is shaky at best (Tjaden & Thoennes, 2000). Additionally, immigrant women who seek assistance from shelters often face language and cultural barriers, and for women out of status, the prospect of seeking potential help from authorities is grossly reduced by the risk of being asked to provide proof of legal residency.

After a few weeks of enduring Morgan's stalker behavior, Wana took a chance and reported Morgan to the police. She appeared in front of a judge after that, to obtain a restraining order against him. Although she remained, in most ways, the same well-put-together, poised young woman, her eyes during those months betrayed a perceptible emotional weariness from worrying about what Morgan might do, regret about marrying Morgan, and a suspicion that perhaps she was not a good person or maybe she was just cursed. Of these worries, the most consistent was her fear of interacting visibly with government officials, any one of whom might ask about her residency. She also worried about the application for residency that she had submitted after she and Morgan were married: Would they disregard it when she filed a complaint about him?

Through contacts of some community-based organizations for immigrants, Wana was eventually able to self-petition for residency as a battered spouse. Apart from this exception, immigrants can only be sponsored by others: established family members who are U.S. citizens or sponsoring companies. Wana did not have a social network of family members who could and would sponsor her application for residency. Although the immigration narrative of this country lauds individuals who come here with nothing and succeed, even from the very nascent stages of immigration, having connections to people who are more established with social and economic capital is crucial. In addition, having established family members with U.S. citizenship is key to being able to step foot on pathways to citizenship. However, even if her stepmother had reconsidered pleas agreed to sponsor Wana's citizenship, Wana had migrated at the age of 16, and once she turned 18, she was too old to be sponsored by another adult. It was from this vacuum of potential sponsors that she sought, somewhat desperately, to create a network that could help her secure inclusion in a stable and safe place in the United States. Fortunately, through the work of the few adults in her life who were knowledgeable about immigration law, resources, and support, Wana was able to access the free legal support that eventually won her a green card. I first connected her with a local immigrant rights group in Boston who provide free legal counseling, and that organization then secured an immigration attorney who had experience with domestic violence cases. Throughout her quest for her green card, she has remained a poised, confident, and exacting young woman, but she has also been more than ruthless in critiquing herself for her past actions. Although she no longer thinks she is a bad person, as she did most acutely when she was looking over her shoulder for Morgan and without any legal avenue for safety from the state, she credits the stability in her life to social workers, advocates, and teachers who helped her. She never notes her own work, perseverance, and resiliency. In this sense, like many who are dispossessed through society, Wana is more likely to apply a judgmental view of meritocracy to herself.

CHAPTER TWO

Lina and Schooling

In the American imagination, education—more specifically, literacy—is the key to both individual and societal success, equity, and achievement. Meritocracy tells us: Work hard, read and write well, and you will be successful. When President Barack Obama was introducing Sonia Sotomayor, his nominee for the United States Supreme Court in 2009, he painted a familiar picture of success, one anchored in this promise of education:

> Sonia's mom bought the only set of encyclopedias in the neighborhood [and] sent her children to a Catholic school called Cardinal Spellman, out of the belief that with a good education here in America all things are possible. With the support of family, friends, and teachers, Sonia earned scholarships to Princeton, where she graduated at the top of her class, and Yale Law School, where she was an editor of the *Yale Law Journal*, stepping onto the path that led her here today. (legaltimes, 2009, para 15–16)

Obama also mentioned Sotomayor's roots as the daughter of Puerto Ricans who moved to the mainland when she was young, in search of a better life. He lauded Sotomayor as a hard worker who had reaped the benefits of a consistent commitment to education. In fact, when a member of a nondominant group achieves a high-profile position within mainstream society, education is invariably named as the key to success. In the United States, policy-based access to a free and public education has been negotiated by various groups and awarded as a symbol of this opportunity. The legal cases of *Brown v. Board of Education* (1954) and *Lau v. Nichols* (1974) are now tropes of the value placed on education as opportunity. Implicit in this opportunity is the belief that an education will afford the knowledge and skills necessary to position youth to be productive, active members of society. When achievement in society is seen as the direct result of hard work, education fits neatly into this view as a primary or even singular space of potential for individuals' and groups' success in society. In fact, national progress in civil rights is almost always evaluated through the examination of equity and inequity within the field of education, as exemplified by a well-known sports metaphor: education can *level the playing field*. For immigrant youth, particularly undocumented youth and those on the boundaries of success and stability, succeeding in education is far from a straightforward matter. This has long been the case for myriad populations of color, beginning with the explicitly colonizing agenda that American schooling had for Native Americans (Lomawaima & McCarty, 2006) and echoing through other poor and racially minoritized populations' experiences (Anyon, 1989; Lareau, 2011; MacLeod, 2009). The example of an immigrant from Niger named Lina demonstrates how people are still acutely differentially situated with opportunities and exclusions within the field of public education.

Lina emigrated at the age of 16 on a tourist visa, at the wish of her mother, who still lives in Niger. Lina's mother envisioned the move as a means of enabling Lina to go to college and achieve a stable professional life, perhaps even as a lawyer. They saved for 3 years to purchase the plane ticket to Boston for Lina.

Lina acknowledges this goal: "She sent me here to do good, to study and become somebody. I kinda wanted to do that, too, you know, to be in America, learn English."

These goals felt possible to both Lina and her mother because Lina's older sister had come to the United States and married a U.S. citizen, subsequently applying for and receiving permanent residency. However, while Lina was in secondary school, her tourist visa expired and she turned 18. Both of these conditions complicated the possibility of residing in the United States with authorized status, and possibly eliminated it altogether. As with Wana, Lina and the other 2.5 million undocumented youth in the nation, when they turned 18 without a family member who coould sponsor them for legal residency, they became undocumented. While Lina and her family knew that being undocumented greatly complicated any wishes for a professional life, what was less transparent to them, and to most immigrants, are the ways in which immigration laws are far from a straightforward matter of age.

Over the years, U.S. immigration policy has fluctuated to reflect both the needs of and perceived threats to the nation. The Immigration and Nationality Act Amendments of 1965 abolished the national-origins quota system and established a categorical preference system. The new, and still current, system provided preferences for relatives of U.S. citizens and lawful permanent residents and, to a much lesser extent, for immigrants with job skills deemed useful to the United States, but it did not abolish numerical restrictions altogether. For some countries (including those from Europe, Asia, Africa, and Australia), the amendments set caps on immigration, as well as a cap for each of the preference categories. Further, the ability to reunify families is limited by certain age restrictions, such as minors needing to be under the age of 18. The amendments are often reviewed formally and changed. The implementation of these laws can be fickle, subject to the perceptions and inclinations of the people involved, which makes an already confusing and daunting set of regulations and practices even harder to decipher.

Under this set of laws, Lina went from being a nonimmigrant in the United States on a temporary visa who could be sponsored by an adult relative (such as her sister) to restriction against applying for legal permanent residency when she turned 18, no matter what the family relationship might be. If she were 16 and still lived in Niger, her sister might have been able to apply for residency for her, but because she had already entered the United States as a minor and then turned 18, this pathway was closed to her. Had she submitted an application for residency, it's also likely that being Nigerian would not have worked in her favor due to the formal policy and the less formal but perhaps even more powerful challenge of being racially minoritized. However, even if Lina and her family had decided to apply for her residency before she turned 18, they would also have struggled to come up with the money that is needed for most residency processes and applications. Lawyers' fees, application fees, and processing fees can quickly add up, with documented immigrants paying between two and five thousand dollars for an individual case. Because undocumented cases are far more complicated, the fees run even higher. Like most people in the United States, the immigrant family members I interviewed, including Lina's sister, saw the splashy ads from personal injury attorneys on television and thought that all attorneys provide services and only collect if granted victory in court. But of course, very few immigration attorneys provide money-back guarantees. In fact, to begin discussing a residency case, most lawyers require a minimum of $150.

By the time that Lina went from holding temporary visa status to being undocumented, she had settled into the United States, her all-immigrant high school, and her community. She had become an essential member of her sister's family, babysitting her two young nieces, one 3 and one 18 months old, while her brother-in-law and sister worked and attended community college courses. Lina's days, while she was in high school, typically began at 5 A.M., when she made breakfast for the family, woke her nieces and sister to get ready for the day, and sometimes attended to some homework on the way to school. Her sister stayed at home with the children during the school day and Lina returned home directly after school to babysit her nieces and cook dinner while her sister worked evening shifts as a nurse's aide and attended her community college course, and her brother-in-law worked in a store. Without Lina's help with child care, which amounted to 30 to 50 hours per week, the family would not have been able to make ends meet on the low-paying wages they earned in service industry jobs.

Conservative estimates suggest that women make up 60% of the low-wage workforce, and as startling as this statistic is, it does not speak to the numbers of women who make no wages whatsoever. There are over 4 million undocumented women in the United States, and most of them perform one or more types of home-based labor such as cooking, cleaning, and child care that goes unpaid. While undocumented males are likely to work in craft, labor, and transportation, undocumented women are more likely to work in service indus-tries of food preparation, cleaning, and child care. Sociologists McLafferty and Preston termed this difference a "spatial mismatch" across genders in 1992, and not much has changed since then.

Lina's graduation from high school meant that she had more time to devote to the family's needs in child care and housework. She continued to do this un-paid household work both because her family needed this role performed and because without authorized documentation status she had few options for paid employment. In fact, one year after Lina graduated from high school, she and her family moved to the Midwest, to afford a better lifestyle. Still, Lina was the person who provided child care and did much of the family's housekeeping. Her family's gendered work roles moved across state boundaries in a way that echoes move-ment of structures and routines across the imaginary boundaries of nations and states. Further complicating this family history is the fact that although increased freedom and opportunity for women moving to the United States from lesser de-veloped nations might be the ideal, it is not necessarily reflected in real situations like Lina's. While there are, without a doubt, better rights afforded to women in the United States, there remains a structured gender inequality. In that system, low-income women are the most vulnerable (Dodson, 2009). In Lina's case, as is the case with many immigrants, her own cultural background of gendered family roles mapped disarmingly well onto the roles afforded to low-income women in the United States, both native-born and immigrant.

As an undocumented young woman with pressing familial financial obliga-tions and few avenues for personal development, after she was finished with school, Lina spent most of her time babysitting, cooking, and cleaning. Lina often expressed frustration at the limits to her work situation, as child care was not in her aspirations for herself. However, she has, as she put it, "made peace with stuff I can't control. If not, I go crazy."

Part of Lina's frustration stemmed from her identity as a student and the fact that, even within the realm of schooling, a promised "even playing field," she experienced firsthand how truly differential access to opportunity was in practice. In her years of schooling both in Niger and in an American high school, Lina excelled in all subjects, particularly writing and composition. She loved ideas and reading, writing, and talking about them. When she found some time in the evenings for herself, after her nieces had gone to bed, Lina usually stuck her nose in a book, sometimes choosing what is colloquially known as "street literature" and sometimes reading more work by authors she encountered in school.

Inside and outside of the classroom, Lina had a strong personality. She was quick to offer insights during discussions, and although she was usually able to support her opinion, she would voice one whether she was able to support it or not, smiling and laughing when she was called out without evidence for her claims. Lina's strong personality emerged when she saw injustices unfolding around her. Voicing dissent from others came easily to Lina, and she often held sway with her peers. For example, when the principal of her high school made changes to the school schedule, conjoining History and English into one class, most students grumbled in the hallways about not having a course dedicated to English instruction, but very few of them did more than disapprove quietly of the changes. Many of the students had come from countries where the educational systems were much stricter, where teachers' authority was respected, and the student's job was to sit and receive didactic instruction. Lina, however, was rarely quiet as a student, particularly when she dissented from the authority's decision, so she became one of the key organizers of a student protest. In the middle of school one day, all of the students marched directly out of the building and into the quad area, holding signs demanding change and demanding to be heard. When the principal joined them and tried to engage the students in a dialogue about what issues they had, Lina was one of the most vocal and direct in speaking back to the principal.

"OK, OK, guys, I know you have some concerns, and I want to hear what they are, but you can't just leave class. Come on, you know better. Now come on, let's get back in there," the principal started moving the students, his arms spread wide, back in the direction of the building. Some of the students started moving that way, but there were also some murmurs of protest.

A small group mostly made up of young women, including Lina, exhibited a lot of eye rolling, teeth-sucking sounds, and murmurs of "See? Told you? Como siempre." Then one in the group nudged Lina with her shoulder, saying, "You go. Talk."

Lina separated herself from the group and stood in a space with some clearing. At 5 foot 9, with long curly black hair and a robust voice, she made a visual impression in her well-worn winter boots, jeans, and hooded winter coat.

"You say you want us to have a voice, and we do, but then nothing changes." Some of the other students started cheering. "You, you just do what you want." Her peers now roared. "We want Mr. Salbado and Ms. W. back," she exclaimed, naming two of the well-loved teachers who no longer worked at the building and making clear the students' disapproval of these staffing decisions.

The issue was eventually resolved, but over the course of this scene and others like it, Lina emerged, sometimes cantankerous and not always well informed, but a clear leader of her peers. She also spoke up frequently at home, with Lina butting heads with her older sister over anything that struck her as unjust, unfair, or unwarranted, from what to watch on TV to how Lina should spend her limited free time.

Lina was developing a sense of maturity and grasp of the larger social picture that motivated her temporary refusals of imposed rules and guidelines. If she had had time to be involved in clubs and afterschool activities, this combination could have been honed into youth leadership traits. More than aware of her quick and sharp tongue, this reflective young woman often softened her remarks or made self-deprecating comments about her straightforward and sometimes combative style. Sometimes as I sat and talked with Lina and laughed with her at stories of temporary clashes with teachers, friends, and family, I could see how Lina could easily have had a life in politics or the law or even broadcasting. But Lina's situation included a prickly combination of strong academic abilities, undocumented migrant status, and heavily restrictive family responsibilities. This combination affected not just Lina's ability to attend college but also became apparent in smaller moments in her education that positioned her less favorably than her peers.

When the school day ended, the students in Lina's high school, like most students, would usually hang out for awhile, catching some time with friends before going off to their various responsibilities. Some, including Lina, had to leave to work, some had to head home because they were expected to be home after school, and others went off to soccer or softball practice. Most of the other top students in Lina's class would gather their belongings and head back into the classrooms to seek extra help. For example, Matthias, an immigrant from Cape Verde, was one of Lina's peers who also received excellent grades. One day I was looking for Matthias after school and found him in his English teacher's classroom. They were both poring over a piece of paper, sitting side-by-side as they worked on the wording of a letter. Both greeted me when I came in, and Matthias asked if I could wait for a few minutes, he would be done quickly and then could work with me on our project. While I waited to speak with Matthias, I gathered that he was getting writing help not for an assignment, but for a solicitation letter for a school-sponsored service trip to the Dominican Republic that he wanted to attend.

"See, Matthias, you wrote here, 'If you can, please help me on this trip. I am thanking you for your help and support of me and the trip,' but you don't provide any reason why they should do this, other than asking," the teacher explained.

Matthias listened intently and then asked, "That's not enough?"

"No, you have to give the readers a reason why they should support not just anyone but you. Who are you giving this to?"

"Oh, I know that!" Matthias grinned largely. "I'm going to ask people who work with my father. I know some of them; they're pretty nice, you know, and my dad said they might help me."

"OK, so great, mention some things that they might already know about you, but remind them. Try this," the teacher took Matthias's pencil, and as she wrote, she read aloud her writing, "As an immigrant who is learning to be a leader, this trip will . . ." The teacher paused, "What will the trip do for you, Matthias? What do you think?"

"Well, it's going to help me work with other people and help other people, you mean like that?"

"Yes! Good, so let's try this again. 'As an immigrant who is learning to be a leader, this trip will help me develop my ability to collaborate with others.' There, can you see how *collaborate* is better than *work with* here? And you have to write about you, it's not like the writing you do in school, like in science. It has to be personal but also sound professional. Do you see that?"

"Oh, yeah, Miss. That's definitely better. Even the way you said *collaborate* instead of *work with,* that's better," He smiled broadly. "I knew you could help me, thanks!"

In one small after-school session, Matthias got a quick but potent lesson in syntax and grammar honed for a particular audience, a set of skills that is essential for effective writing. Lina had this same teacher for her English class and soon after this after-school talk with Matthias, she showed me one of her papers on which she received a C. It was evident that Lina was not happy.

"Ms. K. gave us an assignment and we had to do a rough draft. So I did, and she gave me an A-, telling me to be more descriptive. OK, so I did, and then she gave me a C because she said it *[using finger quotation motions]* 'didn't show improvement from the rough draft.' I just don't get that, you know?"

In that moment, I understood both Lina's frustration at the vague feedback and her inability to improve her grade by asking her teacher for extra help after school, as Matthias had done.

I also understood her teacher's situation. I was not able to elaborate on the instructions to be more descriptive, and I empathized completely with this English teacher who was navigating how to best support the writing skills of 60 immigrant students, which varied widely, almost wildly. Some of the students had had interrupted schooling in their past, some had received only didactic instruction in largely rural areas with little support in the way of books, writing materials, or resources we tend to think of as ubiquitous, such as computers and the Internet. Other students had received strong, formal schooling in the capital cities of their countries. But, for most teachers, as for this one, the prior educational experience of their students is not easily known due to incomplete or missing records and embarrassment of reporting interrupted or lack of formal schooling (Decapua & Marshall, 2010). Most often, this crucial information must be gleaned from one-on-one conversations, which require a trusting youth-adult relationship. All of the educators I know desire to achieve this trust with their students but struggle to find the time and space to build those relationships.

Lina's and Matthias's English teacher was expected to bring all of these students, with their mix of premigration schooling experiences and individual abilities, up to grade-level competencies within an academic school year and prepare them for state proficiency exams. It sounds logical, but the timeline of the academic year is unforgiving of the variance found in most schools but exponentially felt in classrooms and schools with sizeable immigrant populations.

With a teaching load of 60 immigrant students in their senior year of American high school, this English teacher could not give the kind of one-on-one careful editing Matthias received to all of her students inside the classroom-based practices of drafting and revising. The assistance she provided after school was excellent and largely done uncompensated, out of her commitment to her students. Unfortunately, even this extra assistance reflected inequalities in work responsibilities, documentation status, and gender. These inequities, intentional and not, structure significantly different borders for inclusion in society.

While some students were receiving one-on-one help after school, Lina would be on the city bus, making her way home and doing what homework she could finish before starting to take care of her nieces. Taking advantage of educational opportunity, which sounds so simple when we're listening to a Supreme Court nominee's story, quickly becomes a complicated tangle of conflicting responsibilities in stories like Lina's.

CHAPTER THREE

Double Consciousness

Matthias ultimately received a full-ride scholarship to an elite private college whose annual tuition hovers around the $60,000 mark. Matthias is an intelligent and capable young man, but as in many situations, the best rewarded student is not necessarily the one with the most innate ability. Matthias's teachers and peers, while happy for him, were dubious that a student who was not one of the top students of the class academically hit the mother lode of scholarships. For high school teachers, who put in hours upon hours trying to prepare students to be academically competitive for college scholarships, it was a reminder that many factors outside of grades garner favor in scholarships and other rewards.

One of the reasons that Matthias did so well in the status game of college admissions and financial aid was related to the letter in support of Matthias's participation in a high school–sponsored service learning trip that he was revising with his English teacher after school. Matthias's grades were solid, but he had also been on several service learning trips, had volunteered at a local elementary school, and had participated in an intense youth leadership development program. All of these activities exposed him to mentors outside of school, provided him with access to professional-like apprenticeships, and made his college applications more impressive. They also required a commitment of extracurricular time, making them more accessible for some students than others, like Lina.

Throughout the halls of Matthias's high school, and in the halls of my education building on campus, there are pictures, signs, and advertisements for past and upcoming service learning trips. In my university, undergraduates can sign up to journey to places like Natchez, Mississippi, to volunteer at an orphanage during their spring break. Franklin High School's staff have worked to sponsor and chaperone two service trips a year, to the Dominican Republic, Honduras, and St. Croix, among other destinations. Bake sales, lunch sales, and solicitation letters help raise anywhere from a few hundred to a few thousand dollars to help a student participate in the trip.

These trips are somewhat of a hybrid between foreign exchange programs that used to be mostly for well-financed college students and volunteering at a soup kitchen for a day. Combining tourism, service, and social networking, they are growing rapidly in popularity. A Google search for "high school service trips" yields over 8 million hits. A particularly strong offshoot of this cottage industry is the international service trip, in which students "join other globally-minded students on meaningful and exciting teen volunteer abroad programs" (see the website of Global Leadership Adventures, a business that coordinates service learning trips to South America, Asia, and Africa for high school students at http://www.experiencegla.com/). Part of the reason that these service trips have become a business is that colleges and job search committees read these trips as symbols of potential demonstrations of leadership, community service, and international acuity. Where Honor Society students used to try out for a sport or run for Student Council to round out their paper image of academics, students now also hop on planes with a dozen other peers and a few teacher chaperones, to have "meaningful and exciting adventures." But for immigrant youth, phrases like "globally minded" seem odd. Already experienced travelers and border crossers of cultures, the immigrant students I know who have documentation to travel are always attracted to these trips, seeing them as ways to travel more, have fun with peers, and, of course, add information to their resume. However, as is the case in most practices, what happens underneath the surface of rhetoric and framing reveals as much, if not more, about the politics of inclusion and participation.

On one of these trips, sponsored by the high school, I was hanging out with Yveline, a 16-year-old from Haiti, and Radailyn, an 18-year-old from the Dominican Republic. Yveline, Radailyn, and I were on a 10-day service trip to a rural part of the Dominican Republic with 18 other students and teachers. Most of the students on the trip were Dominican, so this service trip was already very different from the more typical service trips undertaken by American students from the suburbs. The small agrarian town we visited had about 500 residents, most of whom were Dominican, although about 15% of the town's population was Haitian. As many as one million native-born Haitians live and work in the Dominican Republic, and they are often subject to racial discrimination and practices of racialized differentiation that date back to Spain's occupation of the nation.

The town where we were staying was about an hour from the more populated, touristy beach areas of the D.R. It boasted two colmados, quick-stop stands where we became frequent and welcome customers, purchasing candy, bottled water, and other items that displayed our status as visitors in the town, where our first and most frequent interaction with locals was buying something. For all of us, but most notably for the Dominican students back in their home country, this also positioned them in a higher class than the town's residents. Although local residents hung out by the colmados, we were the only ones who bought something on every visit, toting our requisite bottles of water.

The two colmados were situated along the three main streets in town, which intersected to form a scrubby, triangular patch of land. This was our home base, and we had been working to transform that intersection into a town center, a park, a square where, as we hoped, the town members could gather and spend time in the evenings, talking, playing ball games, and sharing drinks and chips bought from the colmados. As we started to dig up the weeds in the sandy dirt at the center of the triangle in the first few days of the trip, most of the Dominican residents came out to greet us and have easy conversations about the town. The Haitian population was decidedly more reserved, and they lived at a greater distance from our work area. Most of the Haitians lived in what was colloquially known as the "Haitian Complex," a subsidized housing complex with about three Haitian extended families. The teacher who had sponsored the current trip had also organized a trip the previous year in which students painted the exterior of the Haitian complex. This teacher worked with the Dominican students to dig into family histories and connections to Haiti. Part of his agenda was to prompt the Dominican students to better understand their histories, including the intertwined relationships between the Haitian and Dominican sides of the island, by journeying back to their country, and he facilitated the trips with this in mind, incorporating service work and opportunities for discussion into the overall plan.

When we weren't working on the park, we were staying in a makeshift dorm, all 11 of the females in one room, and the 10 males in another. The girls shared one bathroom and sacked out in cots and bunk beds each night in the large room with a concrete floor. They had a single hand-held mirror that one genius had brought. That mirror ended up being the gathering place in the room, as everyone took turns and gathered around to fix hair and apply makeup, in staunch denial of the fact that it was all bound to wilt in 5 minutes under the heat and humidity of the Caribbean summer. One afternoon, Radailyn, Yveline, and I were back in the room, taking a break from the sun. Radailyn was in front of the mirror. She turned around to catch a glimpse of her backside and saw a tan line on her shoulder.

"Wow, I'm Black!" Radailyn exclaimed in a way that was not altogether negative but not altogether positive either. She had been on her turf since we had arrived here. Her father, who was in politics, had greeted her at the airport, whereas other Dominican families were waiting to reunite with their students until the first weekend, the time we had designated for family visits. Her father had also arranged for the group to have a day at the beach and provided large vans to take us there and back. Radailyn was a popular student in her high school class in the United States, and here that popularity was magnified.

In comparison to other people from the island, Radailyn was relatively light-skinned. When she casually noted the shade of her tanned skin using racialized vocabulary, Yveline, dark-skinned and phenotypically more African than Radailyn, moved her eyes up from the journal on her bed to Radailyn. She looked at her this way for a minute, head still pointed down, but eyes fixed on Radailyn peering into the mirror.

"You're not Black," Yveline said quietly but strongly.

"Noooo," Radailyn said, "I meant it in a good way." She moved away from the mirror and starting sorting some items on her bed, her actions nonchalant as always.

Yveline stayed fixed in the same position and after another long pause, said, "No, I don't think you *did* mean it in a good way."

Radailyn turned around from her bed, bouncing a hairbrush in her left hand. Seemingly surprised that this conversation was still happening, she said, "You should feel good about yourself, have pride in yourself. I do." She was giving a tutorial on self-esteem that Yveline clearly neither needed nor welcomed. Radailyn took note of Yveline's nonresponse, shrugged her shoulders, and smiled at me. "Whatever," she said, as she left the large room. Her laughter echoed back into the room as she made a joke with one of her classmates about the mess in the boys' room. For her, the moment was neither noteworthy nor noticeable. For Yveline, though, their exchange and what she wished she had said hung in the air. She marched around the room, arms akimbo, pointing her finger to punctuate her points.

"Why does she think that I don't have pride in myself? I have pride in myself, but she says, 'Oh look at me, I'm Black,' like, like, aaahh, I don't know, but it makes me mad. I can't even say why but it makes me mad. And you know what? That makes me even more mad."

I understood Yveline, viscerally. That sublimation of emotions into a single frustration was all too familiar. It echoed countless conversations that I had had, that like Radailyn's misplaced lecture about pride were unwelcome.

"Where are you from?"

"No, but where are you *really* from?"

"No, I mean, like, what's your nationality?"

"OK, um, where are your parents from?"

Even at a young age, I couldn't quite fix my mouth to respond to these questions. Somehow, these questions, how they were being asked, and how they deftly positioned me as an outsider and my uninvited interrogator as the insider just felt deeply wrong, and I couldn't begin to put my finger on why. I remembered going to shops with my mother and having various salesclerks puzzle at her accented English and then ask me, the little kid at her side, what she had said. One young woman, who cooed over my mother, saying "I think your accent is soooo cute," looked down and stopped smiling when she saw me, age 6, sticking my tongue out at her. I didn't have the words to express it then, but I knew that my mother had just been made smaller in some way.

Like Yveline, I found it hard for a long time to articulate why this bothered me or why I found it annoying each time I was asked where I was from, even though I had been born in the United States. So I took the obstinate road and answered the questions that were posed to me literally. Although it was slightly more polite than sticking my tongue out at strangers, this was not a completely gracious move either, as the progression of questions usually also accompanied an uncomfortable rising awareness that the right words weren't being chosen. When I did finally just submit and tell people what they wanted to know, the questions and comments got, for me, worse.

"Oooooh, I love India! I think it's so beautiful."

"Oh, no I haven't ever been there, but I really want to go. I love Indian food, and those long dresses the women wear, what are those called? Right, saris, and Bollywood, right? Bollywood is great."

When I was younger, the exchanges were decidedly less enamored coming out of the mouth of most kids, particularly when we lived in mostly White neighborhoods.

"Weird. Why don't you wear that dot thingy on your forehead?"

As in these exchanges, in the conversation between Yveline and Radailyn, Yveline was being forced to look at herself through the gaze of Radailyn, a gaze that simultaneously holds dominance over and amplifies for figurative consumption certain features of "others"—their skin tone, their clothes, their food. For Yveline and other immigrants, these moments and countless others that preceded them and would succeed them, carry the subtle but unmistakable message that first, they are different, an "other," and second, that they will often be encapsulated into a single feature or label, and third, that they do not have full membership or inclusion. Ethnic. Diverse. Exotic. Other.

W. E. B. DuBois first coined the phrase "double consciousness" in 1897 to note the ways in which African Americans are unrelentingly forced to see themselves through both the racist eyes of their oppressors and the societal structures that deny them opportunities. People who are "othered" in society know very well the ways in which their "otherness" (race, ethnicity, class, gender, sexual identity) is often called to attention by the dominant culture. For Yveline, Radailyn's offhand comment about skin tone and subsequent minilecture about self-esteem was infuriating because Radailyn could temporarily enjoy a darker phenotype while maintaining the sociocultural status afforded her, in part, through a lighter shade of skin in her home island, which has been violently divided between racial categories. Yveline also felt deep frustration that her statement to Radailyn denying her Blackness was also a curtailed attempt to make Radailyn aware that while she might grow darker from time to time from the sun, she will never know what it feels like to be racially minoritized in a racist society. Although the history of racial intolerance in the Dominican Republic echoes through many leaders and eras, perhaps the most infamous example is found in la era de Trujillo, when Dominican dictator Rafael Trujillo instituted a harsh policy of anti-Haitianism, exiling anyone with an African phenotype to the Haitian side of the "Plátano Curtain" and legislating a staunch open-door immigration policy for European Jews in the 1930s. These measures conjoined in the effort to whiten the Dominican Republic and remove signs of African lineage from its inhabitants.

In contemporary contexts, conversations about race, ethnicity, and discrimination are at a peculiar juncture. As sociologist Eduardo Bonilla-Silva aptly named the current era, we are living in a time of *Racism Without Racists* (2003). Now that racism is firmly institutionalized through practices that are not explicitly about race but nevertheless organize society according to race, individuals can claim themselves and society to be without racism and absolve any responsibility for a racist society. Much energy is spent in media firestorms debating whether a single comment, tweet, or action is racist, but little attention is paid to the ways in which societal institutions implicitly racialize and organize people.

For example, recent educational policy has been marked by a rising emphasis on—if not obsession with—high-stakes assessment, in which all schools and children are expected to achieve at the same levels (Kumashiro, 2012). While the era of No Child Left Behind required achievement scores to be disaggregated by ethnicity and race, no additional support was provided for low-income schools, which were overpopulated by racially minoritized children whose needs drastically exceed the needs of better monied students in more well-to-do neighborhoods. The result has been a resurgence in the gains of White students over minority students, a phenomenon of converging policy and practice that researcher Zeus Leonardo (2007) has called, "the educational construction of Whiteness." At the same time, zero tolerance policies for drugs in school have led to large swaths of students, mostly Black and Latino, being expelled from school and shepherded in a school-to-prison pipeline. As legal scholar Michelle Alexander details in *The New Jim Crow* (2010), although these drug policies do not specify racial categories as targets, in reality, they systematically sequester racially minoritized populations into prisons. For immigrant populations, prisons are complemented by detention and deportation centers, where there is no such thing as due process (Kanstroom, 2007). In essence, an immigrant with authorization to be in the United States can still be deported just about anytime for a wide array of reasons, from marriage fraud to not notifying the government of a change of address. Those from less economically privileged nations of the Caribbean, Latin America, and Africa, are far more likely to be deported than immigrants from European nations. All of this is happening against a larger more popular discourse that insists that we are a multicultural, postracial nation, one built by immigrants.

However, we rarely have explicit, honest, and even vulnerable conversations about race, ethnicity, and power differences, especially our own, and how those differences structure access to societal status. Even with many Dominican and Haitian students in the same classes at Franklin, conversations about race happened as the students studied writing by Elie Weisel, Lois Lowry, and Chinua Achebe. All beautifully written and moving stories, they did not fully capture the moments in which race and discrimination pulsed through the minutes of these youths' everyday lives. There was a disconnect, perhaps a functionally safe disconnect, between what was studied and what was lived at Franklin. The service trips, as well, often maintained a superficial discussion about community although smaller interactions underneath bubbled with race, power, difference, and conflict. As Matthias attended college, he continued to participate in service trips, this time journeying with his mostly White college peers. I spoke with Matthias one year after he returned from a college service trip to a rural town in Mississippi. I asked him if he noticed any differences across the high school and college service trips.

"No, you know, it's mostly the same. We went down and did some good work, but it was weird."

"Weird how?"

"Well, it was just me and this other kid from New Jersey who were the only Black ones on the trip, and you know me, Miss, I get along with everyone." I nodded in agreement, that yes, Matthias was exceedingly easy to get along with. "But it felt weird because the White kids they were looking like amazed that people live like that."

"You mean in poor conditions? Like their houses?"

"Yeah, everything. The houses, way-old cars, kids running all around. And I felt kind of bad and then like wondering, is that how they look at me? And maybe not the kid from New Jersey cuz he's like them, but I'm Cape Verdean. Do they even know where that is or they just think I'm a poor kid from some other place who got lucky. I wonder if they look at me feeling sorry for me like they looked at those kids."

"And had you thought about that before this trip?"

"Not really cuz on the other trips it was all of us kids who are immigrants. Now it's mixed, and I feel more like I'm watching myself through them."

DuBois' words and ideas are as depressingly relevant for Matthias in this century as when he wrote them almost 150 years ago.

As for the trip to the D.R., we built the park in the middle of the town, patted ourselves on the back, and felt good about our work; but did the trip really increase our global mindedness? In lots of ways, these kids were already more "globally-minded" than native-born youth who haven't felt the push-and-pull dynamics of migration. But what kind of service trip would it take to puncture through easy conversations of teamwork, multiculturalism, and diversity to the more complex but impactful ideas about race, culture, and inclusion?

Filtered through Mary Louise Pratt's (1991) concept of the "contact zone," international service learning trips are an example of "the social spaces where cultures meet, clash, and grapple with each other, often in contexts of highly asymmetrical relations of power, such as colonialism, slavery, or their aftermaths as they are lived out in many parts of the world today" (p. 1). In a sense, we are all living in figurative and material contact zones that don't require trav-el and have been indelibly touched by the histories and trajectories of more privileged cultures preserving domination by keeping less privileged cultures in those places. The most pressing insight of Pratt's conceptual model of contact zones is not in the observation that these zones exist but that they all too often exist without ensuing conversations that productively lift up difference, discord, and conflicts. It's often considered bad manners to talk about politics, religion, or income. Race and racial processes would fall into that category as well, so that by keeping our conversations nice, we also keep everyone in his or her place. What the service trips did for Matthias and Yveline was throw into relief and shine bright lights on the daily ways in which they are racially minoritized. Although they, and most people of color in racially segregated societies like the United States, feel the constant wear and tear of microaggressions and objecti-fication, certain contexts, like the service trips, with their combinations of tour-ism, voyeurism, and service, kick up this awareness to a level of articulation, often frustrated articulation. This is part of the claustrophobic frustration that youth like Matthias and Yveline feel during the moments when they are backed into a flat perception of themselves through someone else's eyes.

CHAPTER FOUR

The Single Story of Adolescence

The American Academy of Child and Adolescent Psychology defines *normal adolescent development* as a stage that occurs in the middle and high school years and is characterized by the following traits: movement toward independence; concern with future interests and cognitive changes; preoccupation with sexuality; and experimentation with morals, values, and self-direction that results in reactions against authority (AACAP, 2011). This guiding model, from the field of educational psychology, connects strongly to and perhaps even reflects the ways we regard teens and adolescents as supremely self-involved, mercurial in their moods, and in opposition to the adults and rules around them. Consequently, conventional wisdom is to bide one's time until those teen years, with their growing pains, are over.

At issue here is not the idea that the teen years can be a difficult time of growth, or that adolescence is qualitatively different from other stages of life. Rather, it is the assumption that the teenage years are the same for everyone and something to be endured, both by teens and the adults around them. These largely unquestioned and widely held beliefs are an example of what author Chimamanda Adichie refers to as the danger of the single story (2009). Adichie, who grew up in East Nigeria, recounts that her earliest writing reflected the "normal" she had learned from British literature. Instead of writing about the tastes and sounds of her immediate life, she replicated the details about ginger beer and small talk about the chilly weather that she found in her British books. Later, her American roommate in college asked Adichie if she could listen to her "tribal" music and assumed she did not know how to use a stove. Adichie's point is that stories have power; they create worlds for us, but they can also have the unintended consequence of artificially circumscribing what is normal and thereby flattening dynamic people and their potentials into static stereotypes. Limiting individuals and even entire populations to a single story dehumanizes because it absolves us of knowing people as three-dimensional and complex humans. For youth, the single story is one of raging hormones, rebelliousness, and defiance of authority. In the context of schooling, assumptions about age, stage, and what is "developmentally appropriate" predominate. As such, a one-size-fits-all perception spurs adults to set limitations that do not always reflect the immediate circumstances accurately.

Matthias bears some strong resemblances to this standard portrait of teen development: His peers are supremely important to him, he is trying to define what his future might be like while working hard as a student, and he has consistent conflict with his father. However, he also exemplifies the danger of the single story. Despite these superficial similarities, the common conception of teen development captures none of the complexity of Matthias's life in the United States.

Matthias was generally seen by his teachers as an excellent student partly because it was commonplace for Matthias to be found after school in his classrooms, at soccer practice, or studying someplace. He was a broad-shouldered, exceedingly courteous young man who was always smiling. Popular with his peers and certainly appreciated by his teachers for his ineffably positive personality, Matthias was one of the most visible students in the school and featured in almost every picture of school functions adorning the hallways.

Because Matthias held U.S. citizenship, he could work fewer hours than many of his undocumented peers, so he also participated in many youth development opportunities. He traveled to China as part of an intense youth development program that mentors youth across their high school years through overseas travel and also participated in Saturday academic programs offered through local universities. While Matthias engaged in these activities because of his academic goals, they also kept him busy outside of the house, which had more to do with his home life with his father than with resumes or college applications.

Matthias had lived with his father since he came to the United States from Cape Verde at the age of 17, and described him as mean, bad-tempered, violent, and always upset. Matthias's father left Cape Verde for the United States 3 days before Matthias was born, splitting from Matthias's mother to create a new life for himself. He returned for 10 days when Matthias was 12 years old, and Matthias remembers these days fondly: "Well, that was different. Everything was wonderful. It was beautiful. He took me here; he took me there. I was happy about him [visiting]. It was like on TV, and that made me excited about the United States and coming here."

Over the years, Matthias's father became a United States citizen, establishing a pathway to legal residency and citizenship for Matthias. With persistent financial and emotional support from his paternal grandmother, as well as the support of his parents, he migrated to the United States at the age of 17, leaving his mother behind and moving in with his father, a virtual stranger. This pattern of family separation and reunification is a familiar one in the lives of immigrants. In the sizeable and growing population of 214 million immigrants and refugees worldwide, as many as 85% of nuclear families experience some aspect of separation and reunification across their migration histories (Suárez-Orosco, Todorova, & Louie, 2002). Additionally, for most immigrant youth, the nuclear family is a mythology; family separation and reunification patterns create what are called stepwise separations, where first a parent or grandparent migrates and then other family members migrate across the years. As one can imagine, this shake-up of family living situations often creates fraught dynamics. Although the research on the effects of these separations for immigrant youth is limited, in a longitudinal study of immigration, young immigrants reported more symptoms of anxiety and depression in the initial years after migrating than immigrant youth who had not been separated from their families, nuclear or extended (Suárez-Orosco, Bang, & Kim, 2010). Matthias, like many immigrant youth, did not show readily visible signs of strain like anxiety or depression as a result of his homelife, but digging a little below the surface showed a complicated history.

One day after school, shortly after Matthias had learned that he had been awarded a full-ride scholarship to an elite private university, we were talking about his transition to college. He expressed fear at the unknown and hoped that he would be good enough to succeed in college but also confided that he needed to get out of his father's home.

"I don't know, Miss, but it's like he hated me from the moment I got here. He tells me all the time that I am not a good son, that he is doing everything for me, and that I don't appreciate it. He tells me that I wouldn't be anywhere or anybody without him." As Matthias spoke of his father, his body tightened. Frequently, in speaking of his father, he shook his head back and forth slowly, conveying that he could not make sense of this harsh and seemingly final character judgment from a man he barely knew but who was supposed to love him. When I asked if there was anyone else in the house who could be a buffer between these two, Matthias smiled broadly, with his trademark quick, wide smile, and told me that his maternal grandmother filled this role in the household. "Oh, yes, Miss, my grandmother is there. I spend a lot of time with her, just sitting with her. I watch her novelas with her, and sometimes I cook for her. I do that for her because I love her and family is family, you know, Miss? I'm not a bad person, so bad. But him [my father], I don't know, I just try to stay out of the way."

It became clearer to me why Matthias spent all of his spare time in classrooms after school and signed up for every youth leadership development program he could find. Although he certainly was a dedicated and hardworking student, he also engaged in these activities to keep himself occupied and out of the house, and to assuage the undoubted impact of his father's words on his psyche.

As Matthias continued to shake his head and state the obvious that he was a good person, I was reminded that this young man is supposedly in the throes of forming his identity, seeking independence from his family, experimenting with morals, and preoccupied with sexuality. I had learned about these characteristics, as do most aspiring teachers, in my university course on adolescent psychology.

These match well with some kids, but are based on a theory of "normal" adolescence established in the early 20th century by educational psychologist G. Stanley Hall, who first defined adolescent characteristics that still predominate in the academic field. Sociologist Nancy Lesko (2001) describes this field of adolescent psychology as itself preoccupied with crises of early and late development. The invention and maintenance of the stage of adolescence has as much, if not more, to do with adult anxiety about people who are no longer children and not yet adults, who occupy a liminality that is socially out of place and whose questioning of authority is, understandably, a challenge for adults. In fact, in Western societies, as milestones like entering and leaving college, securing a full-time job, and getting married shift over time, the ages that are considered to compose the adolescent years have changed, stretching now to include the late teens and sometime even early 20s (Wyn, 2005). Although aspects of the single story of rebellion and independence fit some young people at some points in time, the story shows its limitations quickly, particularly with young people who are not from a European-descended middle- or upper-class background.

Matthias was clearly thinking through what kind of person he was and should be, but his struggle with identity was not limited to the typical example of a teenager pulling away from his parents. Instead, he was struggling with how to reconcile and make meaning of pursuing a stable economic present and future in a new land, striving to be a top student while living with a hostile father who was a virtual stranger and constantly told him he was worthless. By all measures, Matthias was a high-achieving young man: He had a full-ride scholarship to an elite private university, was an excellent athlete, and participated in lots of activities. His teachers adored him, praising him as a polite gentleman and hardworking student. But even in the context of these positive reactions and his many accomplishments, his father's negative messages left Matthias struggling to feel good about himself, missing his homeland and his mother even more, and trying to reconcile his experiences with his father and what it means to be a good man.

Without a doubt, Matthias's father had his own history that contributed to his fraught relationship with his son. Changes in family structure involve recalibrations and adjustments, and sometimes only time and distance can help when tensions reach peak levels. In fact, after Matthias spent his freshman year of college living in the dorms, he returned to his father's house, and the tension subsided significantly. But during his high school years, Matthias exuded tension and stress when asked about his father. In mainstream settings of more typical American high schools, Matthias would likely be assumed to be in a state of rebellious flux. Partly due to Franklin's small size and the experience staff members had with family migration patterns of separation and reunification, Matthias's family situation was known and understood by several adults on the school campus. However, from a more mainstream perspective of counselors and mental health professionals, the primary source in need of intervention would be Matthias, perhaps even exclusively. In short, the single story of adolescence positions intervention attention on Matthias, not his father.

This orientation is problematic on many levels. First, most mental health providers in the United States are native born and have been educated in a Western body of knowledge based in theories of attachment (e.g., Ainsworth, 1989) and grief through physical loss (Doka, 1989). These theories of individuals' cognition and development may not have much relevance to immigrant populations from non-European cultures. Second, this model of mental health support focuses on intervention, with particular emphasis on the youth due to their "adjustment difficulties during the phase of adolescent development," (Crawford-Brown & Melrose, 2001). In other words, the source of difficulties is due to biological age/stage development, and therefore closes off inquiries into contextual factors. This is a subtle but powerful way in which people are excluded from being seen as three-dimensional human beings, with unique contextual factors shaping their needs. In all likelihood, it was Matthias's father, rather than Matthias himself, who was rebelling in this situation. His actions can be interpreted as a reaction against suddenly having an almost-grown man living in his house who relied on him for basic sustenance and parental guidance, which he had no experience at providing; but through the single scope of adolescence as a time of instability, these contextual factors are not pertinent.

CHAPTER FIVE

Lost in Translation

By the time I came to know Rebecca, she was a sophomore at Franklin who worked well with her teachers and was confident in school and growing as a student. She was on the volleyball and softball teams in the high school and her circle of friends included students from several different nations. Among her friends, she often struck a balance between teasing and supporting them. In one conversation after school, which I observed as we were waiting for a bus to take us to a softball game, she warmly chastised Mira and Moksha, two South Asian girls who were also on the softball team.

"Vas a mirar como soy la mejor." Rebecca teased me that I was finally going to be lucky enough to see how good she was on the softball field.

"What did you say? You should say it in English, you know," Mira said, smiling, but still identifying a sore spot for many of the non-Spanish speakers in the Spanish-dominated international school.

"You should learn how to talk in Spanish," Rebecca said.

"Well, you should learn Gujurati," Mira quipped back. "Huh? Why don't you learn Gujurati? Miss speaks both!"

"Because everyone here speaks Spanish, and so you need to know what the people around you are saying. You don't know," Rebecca smiled, "they might be talking about you. Or [bigger smile here and knowing head nod] you might like one of the Dominican boys." Mira laughed shyly as she smacked Rebecca on the shoulder. That was Rebecca: In teasing those around her, she could nail the essence of the situation, but always with a softness that reminded them it was meant in good will and love. She had an ease with what is called *codeswitching* in the linguistics world, of switching between two different registers, creating comfort and ease with her conversation partners, and could do this across many contexts. In fact, this is a common set of skills organically developed in immigrant populations, and particularly young people as they are typically the ones in their families who develop fluency in additional languages through schooling (Pujolar, 2000).

Rebecca came to the United States from the Dominican Republic around the age of 12 with her mother on a tourist visa. Her mother was detained and questioned by the immigration authorities. Thinking that it was her best way to convey her genuine need for safety, Rebecca's mother told the authorities that her real reason for coming to the United States was that she feared for her safety from her abusive husband in the Dominican Republic. She was issued a notice of temporary protective status, pending further investigation. When the court order to appear arrived in the mail about a month later, Rebecca's mother, with advice from her sister, decided it best to avoid any further interaction with the authorities and did not appear. Further interaction with the authorities would bring more questions and scrutiny, she reasoned. She feared that court proceedings would transpire in English only, be led by a judge of unknown power, and include unfamiliar rituals of the court. Now that Rebecca's mother had established a daily routine of working, spending time with her sister, and caring for Rebecca, this blanket of normalcy felt exponentially safer than this vague but dangerous court appearance.

In fact, Rebecca's mother made her decision in a time when deportations have risen, each year shattering the previous year's numbers, with the Obama administration outpacing the Bush administration. In the face of public outcry about families being separated by deportation orders, the White House issued an edict that only undocumented immigrants who are criminals be deported. However, that edict has been followed unevenly at best, with many immigrants who have no criminal records being deported. Although some deportations have been averted for immigrants without criminal records, these cases have coincided with public outcries via social media outlets (Preston, 2011).

In this context, fearing any type of law enforcement is a reality for many undocumented immigrants and is reflective generally of the ways that many populations learn to fear and avoid law enforcement more than develop trust. In a poignant *New York Times* editorial, Nicholas K. Peart (2011) chronicled in vivid detail the ways that many young people of color grow up learning to be vigilant in heavily policed areas. "Police are far more likely to use force when stopping blacks or Latinos than whites," Peart wrote of his neighborhood in Manhattan. "In half the stops police cite the vague 'furtive movements' as the reason for the stop. Maybe black and brown people just look more furtive, whatever that means" (para 6). For low-income immigrant populations, this trepidation, fear, and avoidance of uniformed authority figures is buffeted by an awareness that in more and more locations in the United States, police officers can not only stop people for reasons as subjective as "furtive movements," but then are obligated to demand proof of legal residency. In addition, a little known but powerful part of the Immigration and Nationality Act, section 287(g), authorizes local and state authorities to enforce immigration law. Enacted in 1996 but expanded after September 11, 2001, 287(g) in essence deputizes local authorities and has been adopted in over 70 municipalities, with uneven implementation and significant criticism (Lacayo, 2010). The effect is that in both perception and practice, the power for uniformed and nonuniformed authorities to question and detain immigrants has been amplified. Policies like 287(g) and anti-immigrant legislation in states like Arizona, Alabama, and Georgia have raised questions and criticism of how much the well-established American history of racial profiling has now morphed to target the growing Latino population in the United States (Romero, 2006).

Although most of us would like to believe that the world mirrors *Law and Order* episodes where the good guys work to put away the bad guys and that law enforcement operates for the public good, the reality is that for most of the population, especially the poor and those outside the dominant culture, law enforcement officials are to be feared more than trusted. What we know of institutions like law enforcement comes largely from the information available to us within our immediate circles and therefore echoes differential experiences of society (Alexander, 2010). In just the same way that someone who has never been pulled over by the police and has only sought and received assistance from law enforcement when their rights have been violated might implicitly trust the legal system, in Rebecca's family, more interaction with uniformed authorities could only mean trouble. It is little wonder that most domestic violence in immigrant homes goes unreported and that Rebecca's mother decided not to attend her immigration hearing. If she had had faith, and immediate knowledge, that the rest of the immigration, family court, and deportation systems would act in due accordance with her best interest and on behalf of laws that are meant to protect immigrants who have migrated for a better life, her decision might have been different. For Rebecca's mother, the clearest path to her being able to take care of her family was to continue doing just that and not run the likely risk of being deported and then separated from her daughter.

With that nonappearance, the tourist visas that Rebecca and her mother held were nullified and arrest warrants and deportation orders were issued in their place. From that point on, if either was apprehended and her residency status checked, one or both of them would be detained immediately and most likely deported. This transpired in Rebecca's first year in the country, when she was attending middle school at a school in the Bronx. Although Rebecca and her mother had developed a daily routine of work and school, Rebecca found it very different from what she had anticipated life in the United States would be like.

Rebecca spent the first 12 years of her life in Baní, a district of the Dominican Republic that has a tight relationship of transnational connections with the United States, particularly New York and Boston (Levitt, 2001). As a young child, Rebecca saw adults, mostly men, go back and forth between Baní and their homes in the United States. They would bring American gifts for their Dominican children and wives/girlfriends/mistresses: TVs, DVD players, cell phones, Nintendos, new CDs, and movies. If it fit into a suitcase, it was fair game. Rebecca remembered the time when one of her best friends slowly and carefully doled out Krispy Kreme donuts that her father had given her that afternoon when he arrived from the United States. This friend divvied up the donuts among a lucky few from a circle of about a dozen kids who gathered around to figure out what was in the green- and red-flecked box.

Rebecca, as many other children must, imagined that she would one day also live in the United States and be able to come back for visits sporting "American" clothes, bearing Sony electronics, and showing pictures of her home and car back in the states. The "Americanness" of clothes made in the Philippines and electronics harvested from minerals in the Congo and then manufactured in China is dubious and more than a little ironic. Nonetheless, these material possessions carry an association with American-based prosperity, which scholars term *premigration knowledge* of and experience with the United States. For Rebecca and many other immigrants I spoke to, it simply meant that going to America conferred status.

Once she lived in the United States, she felt anything but cosmopolitan and confident. In her middle school, a typical public middle school with mostly native-born students, Rebecca felt self-conscious about her lack of English, and her Dominican Spanish accent. When she and her mother decided to move to Boston, Rebecca enrolled in the international school. With peers who were all immigrants, Rebecca's English progressed rapidly. She became confident in her speech and her writing, passing the state-mandated proficiency exam on her first try in her sophomore year. In 3 more years she would graduate second in her class. Her newfound confidence enabled her to be that good-humored friend and motivated student with her feet underneath her.

Even while discussing the delicate and difficult topic of being undocumented, Rebecca maintained a sense of humor. I had arranged three meetings with legal aides and lawyers in Boston to discuss their immigration options and accompanied Rebecca and her mother to these meetings. Time and again, they were told that they didn't have any choices except living in the United States as undocumented immigrants or returning to the D.R. As we were visiting agencies and organizations and meeting with legal professionals in their offices, Rebecca was more reserved than she was at school. We were all more subdued. One day, following another unsuccessful meeting with a legal aide, the three of us were waiting for the bus to come around.

"Well, Miss, you see it's just that I don't have that magic number," she said smiling. "But maybe a couple numbers could help; do they give you some to start if you've been good and then maybe more later?"

She and I both chuckled at the idea of being issued half of a Social Security number. This kind of joke only makes sense if you've had to ponder repeatedly that all that stands between you and, say, affordable college or fair work compensation is nine digits.

It can feel arbitrary and surreal. We repeated the exchange in Spanish so that Rebecca's mother could join in on the joke. She did smile but couldn't quite share in her daughter's sense of humor at the serious situation. Rebecca shrugged and put her arm around her mother, assuring her that somehow, things would work out: "'Ta bien, Mamí. Verás."

Rebecca and I had both translated for her mother in the meeting with the lawyer; Rebecca liked for me to be along in these situations, because even though she translated constantly for her family members, she didn't want to miss anything in the meeting with the lawyer. Although her English was far better than my Spanish, it also helped to offset the awkward role that she assumed by sitting with an authority and translating information for her mother. In situations like these, both mother and daughter felt their comfortable roles shift balance. At that moment, Rebecca held more knowledge and, in some ways, more power over that knowledge, while her mother worked to maintain authority and control over the situation even though she was not in control of how the information came to her. This is a familiar immigrant experience, now packaged by Hollywood in the film *Spanglish* (Brooks, 2004). But these translation experiences, called *language brokering*, are far more complicated than a simple exchange of language. As language and education scholar Marjorie Faulstich Orellana has chronicled through her years of research with immigrant youth and children, translation is never neutral. As Orellana (2009) puts it, although we think of translation as the simple and benign task of substituting one word for another, it always involves culture, power, and identity. For many immigrant youth like Rebecca, the untallied economic work that they do for their families and public agencies as translators is vital. They are the ones to fill in forms such as credit applications, apartment leases, and food subsidy paperwork. They read English books aloud to younger siblings. They are, in essence, el mano derecho, the right hand of their families (Orellana, 2009).

One day, Rebecca told me her stepfather, also a Dominican immigrant, wanted to talk with me. After she saw my confused face because I had only spoken with her mother, she clarified for me that her stepfather wanted to talk with me about my work with her and perhaps about college. "I think he just wants to thank you for helping me and stuff. I don't know," she said. In my work as a researcher doing participatory work with immigrant populations, I spent a lot of time with the parents, aunts, uncles, and grandparents of these youth. I was used to visiting their homes, being served some of the best manioc, strong black sugary coffee, and pollo guisado, over which we talked about how hard the kids were working and what they should do after high school. This time, though, Rebecca's stepfather, Christian, wanted to meet before he went to work one day, so we met at a Dunkin Donuts.

Christian and I shook hands. Most of the time when I met the sisters, grandmothers, and mothers of my students, we would kiss each other on the cheeks to greet each other. That was also the case with some of the male family members, but only after I had known them for some time and it felt appropriate. It most definitely did not feel appropriate as Christian and I met for the first time. The three of us sat for a few minutes, with Rebecca looking at her feet through most of the conversation. I started by telling Christian how much I liked Rebecca and thought her to be a bright, talented, and wonderful young woman, and he agreed with me, adding seriously that he wanted to support her. He told me that she wanted to become a doctor and asked me how to make that happen, affirming that he would do whatever it took to help her become a doctor. As carefully, and respectfully as I could, I explained that without access to federal financial aid, from which she was barred as an undocumented student, Rebecca would face a very long road in becoming a doctor, taking the one to two classes at a time that she could afford to pay for at the international student tuition rate. When Christian said that he would pay, I explained to him that full-time international student rates at a state school would cost about $10,000 a year.

"Sí, pero algo debe cambiar." "Yes," he agreed, "but something must change," and mentioned being more hopeful "con el Obama." I sympathized with his plea; an obviously smart, hardworking, and dedicated student should have the ability to continue attending school. Although the election of President Obama, which had taken place about one month before this conversation, was initially hopeful for lots of immigrants, the record-breaking number of deportations under this administration, 400,000 in its first two years, minimally gave pause for thought. Looming promises of immigrant law reform sat alongside complex codes, decidedly more complex than tax law, and the complexity did not swing in the favor of low-income young immigrants. Even Obama's executive order of June 15, 2012, only adds a bandaid to a deeply flawed constellation of policies and practices, failing to address access to higher education, extend social welfare to precarious immigrant families, or establish a pathway to citizenship. Added to the complexity of the law is the rising tide of xenophobia across the nation, in which suspicion of being an immigrant is increasingly license for officials to question and detain individuals. For young people like Rebecca, immigration law reform would need to comprehensively address societal institutions and institutionalized racism and establish a pathway to citizenship.

For the immediate purposes of the meeting with Rebecca and Christian, though, the fact was that without any sweeping policy reform, Rebecca's chances of obtaining a college degree were slim, and of becoming a doctor, miniscule. As her stepfather and I discussed what options were realistic currently, what change might bring one day, and what to do in the meantime, Rebecca was silent. It was one thing for her to console and joke with her mother; to engage in this conversation with her stepfather, clearly the primary authority in her new nuclear family, was unthinkable. He had set up this meeting to establish his desire to help her, and he was doing that from the position of a patriarch, who should rightly be able to order and organize his immediate world. Rebecca also knew that it was difficult and frustrating enough for her stepfather to be told by this younger female professor that from his position as the head of the family, he was nevertheless powerless to help her, which he saw as his duty. It would only add salt to the wound if she interjected in the conversation, even though she might well have better understood her possibilities and limitations. Rebecca's experience is echoed in many young immigrants' experiences of knowing more about the educational system than their parents (Feliciano, 2006; Gandára & Contreras, 2009) When we reached the end of our conversation, Christian stood up to leave and we shook hands again. Rebecca whispered a quiet "Gracias, Miss" as she followed her stepfather out of the donut shop.

The story of Rebecca and other immigrant children who are language and cultural brokers offers much for us to learn and build from. The field of child psychology, working from a singular story of family that Adichie (2009) warned against, has tended to pathologize language brokers by interpreting their childhoods as problematic and looking for the harms incurred when children translate for others. From a different view, though, it is problematic itself to imply that immigrant youth should summarily not be translating for their families and social agencies, as reality belies the relevancy of these questions. These inquiries are often premised on a mythical [American] nuclear family in which children don't have any such responsibilities and are therefore left to develop as children only. Additionally, these inquiries also position language and cultural brokering as damaging to children and youth (Tuck, 2009). Rendered invisible is the stockpile of linguistic and cultural acumen that immigrant youth develop through assuming the role of interpreter. Immigrant youth who translate for others are keen observers, aware of subtle nuances of power and position, and often diplomatic in their mediation between entities. An English composition lesson on point of view is rudimentary for this population. Rather than begin from an assumption that students need to be taught skills and content as if they have no repertoire of related knowledge, we would do better to know the skills that they are bringing with them and build from those. Without this, particularly against the backdrop of a nation that is rapidly transforming demographically with the growing Latino and Asian populations, we are literally losing vast amounts of potential. Minimally, tapping into the skills of immigrant youth would provide opportunities to revise and update views of youth development that do not speak to all young peoples' experiences, skills, and offerings.

In Rebecca's case, the single story of adolescence obscures our ability to recognize and build on the abilities and skills that some youth may hold, simply because it doesn't fit within our already prescribed understandings of youth characteristics and needs. In other cases, such as Matthias's and his father, the single story of adolescence obscures a more comprehensive view of family conflict. As Adichie (2009) points out eloquently, "The single story creates stereotypes, and the problem with stereotypes is not that they are untrue, but that they are incomplete. They make one story become the only story."

CHAPTER SIX

There's Learning and Then There's Schooling

For youth, school is a central place in their lives. Although most adults see school primarily as the place where learning is supposed to occur, for youth, it is much more than courses and textbooks. It's one of the primary places to meet other kids, build a daily routine, and, with any luck, have a mentor or caring adult who notices when they don't show up.

Franklin High's staff, like any educators worth their salt, strove to provide their students with homes away from home both in the sense of the American home where they now rested nightly and their previous home countries that they had left behind. In their view, the school should be a place where students can be safe and secure and learn. This mission, commonplace as it is, is hard to achieve despite the millions of dollars pouring in and out of educational research projects. Like Supreme Court Justice Potter Stewart's decree about pornography—that it's hard to define but you know it when you see it—it is likewise difficult to define. But Franklin High had it. It was not uncommon to find teachers and students working before and after school every day of the week, as Matthias did while receiving extra help on his service trip letter. All of the administrators knew each and every single student by name and knew their family backgrounds as well as the conditions of their migrations to the United States. Most of the school's staff was bilingual, and many of the teachers were immigrants themselves. In terms of professional principles of caring and the personal knowledge to back it up, it doesn't get much better than this.

In the time students spent in the school, the staff worked to prepare them for graduation, which meant they had to pass the state-mandated high school proficiency exams in English, math, and science. By the measures of high school completion and passing rate on these proficiency tests, the school was phenomenally successful. In a time when a 50% dropout rate was not uncommon for an urban public high school, and around 20% for immigrant populations (Childtrendsdatabank, 2011), Franklin graduated close to 90% of its students and about the same percentage passed the state proficiency exam. However, it would have failed the federal guidelines of adequacy for public schools, which mandate that high school be completed in 4 years or less. Franklin often worked with the students for 5 or 6 years instead of the standard 4, as this helped the students learn standard English in addition to the required academic content and develop the confidence necessary to pass the high school proficiency exam and think realistically about life after high school. Even those students who stayed for more than 4 years required many hours beyond the regular school day to become proficient enough to pass the state exams and graduate.

If the enormity of this task for everyone involved at the high school doesn't seem amazing to you, imagine that you have just landed in a foreign country. You are 15 years old. You don't speak the language fluently, or much at all. You rehearse how you are going to phrase and pronounce your request to the cashier behind the counter before you approach her and you are invariably puzzled at the rapid and unfamiliar response you get. After a while, your ears might start to discern and understand the slang and accents you're hearing, but for a long while, it's simply incomprehensible.

As an immigrant youth, though, you've got to participate in your classes and most likely carry the weight of translating for your family. By the time you've picked up the necessary phrases for shopping, health care, and social service interactions—probably faster than others in your family—you're still at a "nonproficient" level of language fluency as far as the state is concerned. You've got just a few years to learn differential equations, the process of mitosis, the characteristics of prokaryotes, and the difference between *pathos* and *ethos*—in English, and academic English at that. You have to know how and why to write a sentence like "The noxious variety of musk thistle proliferates rapidly," rather than "That weed is messing up the garden."

This was where the staff at Franklin High School came in, working diligently and taking very seriously their goal of getting their students to the same level of proficiency that native-born youth in public and private schools must meet to graduate from high school. However, most of the adults I knew in that school took equally seriously their charge to know the students well enough to contextualize educational goals with the students' socioemotional needs. Although all of the administrators in the school knew each of the students, their family backgrounds, their documentation status, their attitudes toward school, and whom they're dating, none of this information was systematically kept in a database. The only information about each student stored in the public school database was the country of origin, date of entry into the school system, and scores on a few standardized assessments. The rest came from interpersonal knowledge, built on a daily basis, of the students and their families. Because all of the administrators were bilingual and had years of experience working with and living within immigrant communities, building this knowledge was a natural endeavor for them. They, as well as many of the teachers, met one-on-one with students, talked with their parents, and saw the students interacting with their friends at lunch and before and after school. All of these interactions created the foundation upon which students were known well by some school staff.

For other teachers, though, knowing the students this well was more challenging. Teachers are trained to interact with students primarily in classroom settings. Teacher preparation programs focus on learning objectives, the philosophy of education, and various methods of teaching content areas. Immigrant students are not specifically discussed, but English language learners are, and mountains of approaches and methods exist to help these ELLs (like all professional and bureaucratic fields, education is replete with acronyms) learn English quickly and accurately. Once they are working in schools, teachers must focus on their state-mandated curriculum to get students ready for the state proficiency exams, and this is where the space for interpersonal interactions starts to narrow rapidly, dizzyingly. For example, as a science teacher, you would need to possess not just content knowledge about musk thistle, but also how to teach about it in a way that is engaging, builds schematic knowledge of plant biology, attends to various students' linguistic and cultural knowledge and experiences with scientific content, addresses an academic language objective that is not just about vocabulary, and make sure this teaching also prepares students for their mandated assessments in science. And that's just one lesson.

The structure of schooling, then, has logically, although regrettably, reflected priorities of content over relationships. Despite the small size of Franklin and the exceptional closeness between the adults and students, students were not known or understood uniformly across the school. As with most other contexts involving many human dynamics, relationships were uneven, with some teachers, more than others, struggling to know the students well.

Mr. Knox is one example of a teacher for whom connecting with his students was far from a given. A monolingual White man in his 40s, he came to teach at Franklin High with about 10 years of experience working with secondary school students in more mainstream public schools. He had high energy and was determined to engage his students in creating personal connections to reading and writing using technology. His heart was, as they say, in the right place, and he cared deeply for his students. High strung and sometimes shrill in his admonitions and praises to students, his demeanor stood in sharp contrast to the more classically machisto young Afro-Caribbean and Latino males in his class who wore baggy pants, sported large cubic zirconias in their ears, and glowered dramatically if anyone was taking a picture with their phone anywhere nearby. Although the students didn't quite understand Mr. Knox, they liked him because he always opened up his computer classroom for the students during lunch and before and after school. Even during those downtimes for Mr. Knox, he would constantly move from student to student, helping kids insert a graphic into their presentation, animate a slide, edit an audio excerpt, or access a site that had been blocked by the district's Internet policy. Mr. Knox's classes weren't the most challenging for the students. In fact, they felt pretty basic in their requirements that students produce word processing documents, database spreadsheets, and presentation slides. The students liked best, and moreover respected, the teachers who challenged them, were consistent in their grading and discipline, and taught them difficult content. But even with his foreign-to-them mannerisms and easy class, the students generally enjoyed Mr. Knox and did well in his class. So I was surprised when Magdana, a bright young Haitian student in her 3rd year in the school, confided in me that she was having trouble in Mr. Knox's class. When I asked her what the problem was, she said she didn't want to do the "journey" assignment. Mr. Knox had directed the students to create a slide presentation that told the story of their journey to the United States. I had seen several students working on their presentations after school and had helped a few of them with the images, wording, and ideas for the assignment.

"I don't want to do it," said Magdana plainly.

"Because?" I pushed for a little more information.

"Have you been to the class when we have to present it?"

Not only had I not been to the class, but I did not know that students were expected to present their work. Oral presentations were common in the school, used as a way for students to work on their English fluency in public zones and celebrate achievements in learning. But with migration stories, particularly in a school with so many undocumented students, sharing journey stories was not as straightforward as it sounds in a lesson plan book. It was, in fact, risky to share this type of personal information, and therefore basic survival strategy dictated that undocumented youth guard their stories. Because the details of being undocumented had simply not been part of what Mr. Knox had known in his life, and because teacher preparation tends to focus far more on curriculum content than the contexts of students' lives, this impactful reality was understandably beyond his experience. I asked Magdana, who was undocumented, if sharing her journey was her only objection.

"No, it's not just that, Miss. Some people went yesterday and presented. Well, they did theirs, but first he [Mr. Knox] told us that we have to listen to everyone and share in their story. I didn't know what he meant, but then when some people presented, they got a little upset. And they started crying, and Mr. Knox was kind of crying, too. I think you get a better grade if it has more feeling, more emotional, you know? But I don't want to tell everyone my business there."

"Yes, of course. You should not be telling anyone about your situation unless you know you can trust that person," I told her. "But I'm not really sure that people need to cry for you to get a good grade . . ."

"Yes, Miss, they do," Magdana interrupted me. "You know how Mr. Knox is, he likes it when we are very personal and share a lot of ourselves, and if we cry, it must mean that it's more personal. So I need your help." I could see where this was going, but I asked Magdana how I could help.

"I need to do the assignment. I want a good grade. I don't want to tell the truth. What do I do?" Magdana and I both knew that she needed to bluff her way, at least partially, through the assignment. She was, in essence, asking for some company and help, as hers was the only migration story she had, and it was not an option to share it openly.

So, for the next few minutes, Magdana and I mapped out a presentation with a fake journey story for her, one that included some difficulties along the way but that ended more or less happily with Magdana living with her uncle in Hyde Park. When our initial plan for the presentation didn't include enough dramatic difficulties, like saying goodbye to extended family and friends, Magdana protested that it was too neat, that it needed something. When we added in a few based-on-someone-else's-true-story details of hardship, Magdana's eyes almost sparkled.

"This is good, Miss! He's gonna love it. I knew you could help me." She then laughed as I hung my head, shaking it in disbelief that I was aiding and abetting her less-than-forthright story of migration from Port-au-Prince to Boston.

In addition to highlighting what is not often transparent from a native-born perspective, Magdana's journey story illustrates the difference between "studenting" and learning. She learned more about getting around the assignment to get it done than she did about storytelling and technology, undoubtedly the concepts that Mr. Knox had hoped to teach with the project. She had adapted her knowledge and skills to suit what she thought the teacher was looking for. This made her a good student but not necessarily a learner in this particular situation. In fact, being a good student requires learning the style and expectations of the teacher; Magdana knew both from Mr. Knox's teaching personality and the other students' presentations that hers had to have an emotional impact drawing on stereotypes of migration journeys.

Studenting is necessary and not in and of itself harmful. Knowing how to take standardized tests, for example, is an essential skill for academic achievement but not indicative of innate ability or learning skills. As an educator, I want all my students, including the youth I work with, to be savvy students who know how to ascertain what kind of academic performance is required of them in different situations. Especially for these young people, who have neither the time nor money to afford college test prep courses, explicit help in studenting is vital. When I helped Magdana to "student," it was in service of her academic standing. However, I also want my students to be cogent learners who can adapt to new information and ideas and grow as people. Within the structures and patterns of schools and classrooms, though, all too often the most ardent, dedicated, and painstaking learning is not rewarded.

Right after Magdana presented her journey story, Elvis stood up to present his. When he did, before he could say a word, roars of applause and chants of, "Elvis! Elvis! Elvis!" exploded in Mr. Knox's room. Mr. Knox, smiling, quieted the students down and waited for Elvis to load his presentation onto the laptop. Elvis was one of the cubic-zirconia-earring-wearing Dominican young men in the school. Husky and darkly complected, like everyone in his extended family from Baní, he had two faces: a stern countenance and the good-natured smile that he often sported after teasing a classmate and momentarily derailing the lesson of the day. But Elvis was the kind of kid that only the truly unhappy teachers could ever have a serious issue with. He was simply too kind-hearted. He was immensely popular with his peers and adults and was also a stellar DJ, automatically chosen to DJ for all of the school's events. He also provided the soundtrack for the choicest gatherings of *cyphas*, impromptu spoken-word gatherings that met in the basements of the triple-decker houses in and around Dominican populated streets of Dorchester.

Elvis was the embodiment of charisma, good intentions, and musical talent. He was not, however, a good student. He had, like his peers, made great strides in English by his senior year in high school, when he presented in Mr. Knox's class, but this had cost him even more hard work and sweat than many of his friends. He had attended summer school one year, endured lower level books about simplistic subjects, and logged countless hours in the science teacher's classroom trying to master the mystifying vocabulary and concepts of chemistry and biology. The science teacher, Ms. Rojas, could not speak highly enough of Elvis. This teacher, whose students had gone on to become professional scientists, counted Elvis among her favorites because it was as though every point he earned on a test could only be gained through pain, sweat, and suffering. And he showed up for it again and again. In fact, in those afterschool sessions, it was hard sometimes to tell who wanted Elvis to succeed more: Elvis or Ms. Rojas. It was even harder to tell which of the two Elvis was working so hard to please. This kind of reciprocal commitment also is one of those good school qualities that you know when you see but can't convert into measurable criteria.

Elvis's presentation of his journey story was, unsurprisingly, a smash success. Although no one cried, there was lots of laughter and a few, "aaaawwws," as Elvis showed pictures of his younger primos that he had left behind in the D.R., as well as some head bobs in time to the music clips that fueled his presentation. Elvis said few words, punctuating the slides and music with phrases here and there, but it was an image- and sound-heavy presentation, as he still felt shy about his oral skills in English. He had passed the state-required assessment of oral language fluency in English, which is required of all nonnative speakers; but even after repeated attempts, he could not master the English exam, with its comprehension questions about excerpts from the *Aeneid* and *Oliver Twist*. Since he didn't pass all the required test components—although he passed the math and science portions of the state-mandated proficiency exams—Elvis was not granted a full high school diploma.

The truth is that Elvis was never very fond of school; it was not the place where he felt comfortable, although he made classrooms more comfortable for himself and others by injecting humor where he could, endearing everyone to him. Had he been born into a different social class, Elvis would most likely be in politics, with family support shepherding him through the state-mandated tests. Elvis is now, as was the case during his years at Franklin High, working full-time as a baggage handler at Logan Airport and occasionally spinning as a DJ. Elvis was by no stretch of the imagination a super student. He is, however, a studied and excellent learner, particularly of people and of contexts. You cannot be a successful DJ without knowing your catalog, the scene that you're in, and moving the rhythm of that scene deliberately with music. But, even in terms of deejaying, Elvis experiences borders; without a snappy website, friends with more status, and proficiency in accentless English, he is confined to spinning at the gatherings of his friends and former school, none of which pays very well or leads to gigs in other social circles.

In my job as a teacher educator, I work with some adults who are planning to be educators and others who are already teachers, and all are anxious about adequately meeting the needs of immigrant students, or as they are referred to in education, English language learners. These educators have lots of questions, as they should, about how to teach academic English to newcomers to this country. When they ask me what the best methods and assessments for working with immigrant students are, I think about Mr. Knox and Magdana, about how much there is to know about immigrants and how much lacking that knowledge can undermine all of the student-centered assignments—about how there is no substitute for knowing your students and their social contexts. I also think of all of the bureaucratic and curricular constraints that get in the way of good teachers like Mr. Knox having plenty of disposable time to truly get to know his students, to move past his own experiences in this country and get to know theirs. Some teachers are able to do this, but it is largely through their immediate rapport with students and time spent on out of classroom lessons building their trust. These are skills that cannot be conveyed in a teacher education program obsessed with five-step lesson plans. In teacher education programs, we tend to focus on how to create good learning environments in classrooms, but we don't often differentiate between pursuing the completion of an academic task and genuine learning. This culture of teacher education, nested in a high-stakes assessment arena, makes for an almost constant conflation of studenting with learning. In Franklin High and across the country, great teachers are buried under state requirements, and in turn bury their students under objectives and assessments. This results in teachers who have worked with immigrant students for years but don't know which ones are undocumented and which ones aren't. Due to the structure of schools, they end up serving the purposes of schooling rather than teaching, in which the business of administering flat assessments and quantity of time logged in the building supplants more authentic pursuits of genuine learning. Most of the teachers I know are well aware of this reductive scope of their work and mourn the more dynamic role of a teacher that was their intent for entering the profession.

When my university students ask me how to best work with English language learners, I think of Elvis and how little of the toil and effort in education and schooling translates into achievement, even for documented immigrants, which Elvis was. I think of how a person has to have the right connections, the right way of talking, looking, and acting, and not a little economic momentum to move up rungs on the ladder of social mobility. Mostly, though, I think that when it comes to these youth and their teachers, solely learning English is among the least of my concerns for them, for two reasons. First, I have yet to meet an immigrant for whom learning English is not a worry if not a constant site of effort. Most of the youth I know work diligently to not be perceived as less intelligent, as often is the case when someone speaks with an accent in standard academic English in this nation. Second, even with mastery of standard academic English in hand, inclusion and success in society hinge on many more interlocking factors, factors seen at work in the lives of youth such as Elvis, Lina, and Wana. I worry more about how decontextualized requirements, like "on-time" graduation, reflect very little of their actual learning and even get in the way of the learning that these students need and can demonstrate.

In my work with my college students studying to be teachers, I try to get them to think about this difference between schooling and learning. I ask them to write about the last time that they learned something. Not a time when they studented—figured out the requirements to get the best grade and went after it—but when they learned, actually felt discomfort, dissonance, and even pangs of failure because they did not have the knowledge, the skills, or whatever was needed in that particular context. Students usually write about nonschool events, for example, learning to do a grab-and-jerk move in a weightlifting class, learning to save a drowning person to become a lifeguard, or learning to drive a manual shift car. This is part of the challenge that schools face: Their context is confined, perhaps by their own doing, to tasks that can be taught and completed in a square room with desks and chairs in 50-minute segments. *Dissonance,* the distinct, embodied destabilization that occurs when we are genuinely puzzled by new information or new demands, is essential to learning but difficult to manufacture day after day within these four walls. It is not impossible, though. One of the many challenges that education faces, particularly in a time when greater incentives and sharper negative consequences are tied to students' test scores, is disambiguating school-defined studenting and genuinely arduous learning that makes a person grow in confidence and skill.

In one of these college conversations about studenting and learning, a man wrote that when his daughter was born, there was so much he didn't know that he didn't even know where to begin; he didn't know how to make her stop crying or even why she was crying. While he slowly learned the skills of caring for an infant, some through gross trial and error and some through his wife and mother showing him what to do, he also learned to worry a lot more about what other things he didn't know that she would need from him later. How would he learn these things? He wrote that the experience reminded him, on a daily basis, to both be humble and learn from every possible source. One of the students in his college class, in contrast, wrote about how she learned new information in her college physics classes that had never been covered in her high school physics class. While both of these experiences might in fact count as learning, the young man's experiences are a far more compelling example of how he integrated new knowledge about parenting and changed his practices as an active learner in this context.

In the interest of immigrant students or any group of students who are systematically marginalized and face many different kinds of challenges and obstacles to success, no teacher preparation program can begin to fully prepare teachers in training before they enter schools. Having teachers who are good learners, though, would go a long way.

CHAPTER SEVEN

There's a New Sheriff in Town

Throughout my 6 years at Franklin High School, I worked with the school's principal, a man of impressive, awe-inspiring, and sometimes almost scary energy and speed. Mr. Ojeda always moved, spoke, and thought faster than almost anyone around him. Sometimes I felt dizzy from his rapid-fire speech, which was replete with educational jargon and acronyms about the changes that needed to happen in the school. Even as an experienced education professor, where verbiage is the stock in trade of knowledge, I was often dumbfounded by the barrage of education-ese that Mr. Ojeda could unleash. Here's a typical conversation that happened as Mr. Ojeda was on his way to a classroom:

"Leigh, do you have any research or resources on accountable talk or book sets? *[Aside to a student:]* Euridio, hey man, I got your note, we'll talk at lunch, OK? Don't be late to Mr. M.'s class. *[Back to me:]* The teachers need to be doing more with accountable talk in their classrooms, and this could help them. Do you have anything that you can provide for us? *[Greets another teacher:]* Hey, Ms. G., how is everything going today? You look great. Doesn't she look great, Leigh? So, yeah, Leigh, I think this is really what we've been needing to get to that next level, you know?" This was all said so quickly that I'm not sure Mr. Ojeda even took a breath.

While I was still trying to figure out what "accountable talk" actually meant, Mr. Ojeda had already set a time and day for us to sit down and talk more about it. Some days, I felt like Franklin was Mr. Ojeda's world and I was just along for the ride. At the same time, this man knew all 200 of the students in his school, where they lived, who they lived with, who they had left behind in their home countries, whom they were dating, how much they worked, and where they needed to be challenged as students. You can only know people that well by doing it deliberately, and I suspect that, in Mr. Ojeda's case, this was also the only way he could know the students: as people who were also defined by their roles outside of school as sons, daughters, workers, caregivers, siblings, boyfriends, and girlfriends. Anytime I felt frustrated by Mr. Ojeda's seemingly endless supply of new initiatives, diagrams, and reforms, all I had to do was see him interact with the students. The son of Dominican immigrants, he understood much about the range of responsibilities, skills, and challenges that immigrant youth held. Mr. Ojeda hired teachers and staff who could connect with the students, and while he had a tense history at times with his staff, his central concern was always for the students and their development. Even though the teachers at Franklin did not always see eye to eye with Mr. Ojeda, there grew a collaborative exchange of ideas that helped to create a highly successful student support system.

After 6 years of leading the school, the time came for Mr. Ojeda to leave for a different job, and we met our new headmaster with a great deal of caution and worry. For educators in particular, individual school leaders can greatly impact the tenor and daily practices of a school, for better or worse. Since many of the teachers had worked to establish a positive working relationship with Mr. Ojeda over several years, the prospect of meeting a new leader brought, at a minimum, trepidation.

As we filed into the conference room to meet her for the first time, Ms. Khoury, who was sitting alongside two upper level district administrators, greeted everyone with a purposeful smile and nod. She was an immigrant, and told us so in that first staff meeting: "I know these students. I understand. I am an immigrant myself. I came to this country when I was 27 years old, with my husband. We came here so many years ago, worked very hard, and now we are both successful."

Her words raised a red flag. Her immigrant experience was perhaps light years apart from those of Franklin's students; some of them did not choose to come to this country, others came by themselves to familiarize themselves with blood strangers, and still others were trying to work hard even though the spoils of the American dream were beyond their undocumented reach. Ms. Khoury immigrated as a married adult, and both she and her husband held college degrees and enough cultural and economic capital to facilitate an authorized migration from Lebanon to the United States decades ago. Although she equated her own experience with the students', you could park several hundred Buicks between her story and those of recently immigrated, low-income, and undocumented youth from the Global South. In fact, Ms. Khoury was gesturing toward a false narrative of "the immigration experience" as defined by a single set of circumstances. Frequent references to "the immigration experience" in both research and mainstream circles suggest that divergent journeys, gains, losses, and structures of migration are commonly shared and understood. Without a doubt, immigrants share the life-changing experience of leaving their homes behind and working to create new ones. But outside of that, more differences than similarities texture those experiences. For some immigrants, for example, the journey out of their home country is accomplished through bureaucratic mechanisms and supported by financial and personal resources. For others, it is a struggle of long-standing deprivation, suffering, and response to market forces that pull human resources from less developed countries to postindustrial ones. There's an apt phrase used by many people who work in the field of autism that if you've met one person with autism, you've met one person with autism. The same might be said for an immigrant. Immigration experiences are as varied as humans are, and Ms. Khoury's conflation of her own story with those of the low-income youths at Franklin was concerning at the very least.

Her story of migration also invoked the highly problematic view that personal and professional prosperity is possible in the United States for those who work hard enough. This axiomatic belief is found across all social sectors and maintains a wickedly tight hold as the primary, simple explanation for societal status, with people who are successful equating their success to their own individual efforts, and in parallel fashion, those without resources sure that it is due to their own personal flaws, as Wana and Lina did. Likewise, although education is often held up as the most promising social institution for leveling economic and social differences, the reality and extant research shows that education does more to reproduce social differences than ameliorate them. Said in the context of a school, as a school leader, Ms. Khoury's Horatio Alger story flattened the complexities of advantage and achievement into this simplistic formula. This was the second red flag.

Ms. Khoury was what is called a "turn-around principal," someone who has established a reputation for being able to come into a struggling school, clean house, and get the test scores up. Before coming to Franklin, she had been the principal of a pilot school for 10 years, during which time she revamped it from a run-of-the-mill public school into a pilot school with a more clearly defined mission. The policies of both the Bush administration and Obama administration have shown limited tolerance for schools with low scores on standardized tests. No Child Left Behind, the educational policy initiated under the Bush administration, mandated that test scores be disaggregated by race, ethnicity, language background, and gender. This helped to shed stark light on the failure of public schools across the nation to educate students with African American, Latino, immigrant, and indigenous backgrounds. Later, with the Obama administration's Race to the Top initiative in 2010, states were required to identify their lowest performing schools in economically challenged communities and transform those schools using one of four intervention models: (1) the dismissal of at least 50% of the teaching staff; (2) the conversion of the public school into a charter school; (3) a complete shutdown of the school; or (4) a transformation and reform of all the school's practices, led by a new principal. In essence, Race to the Top mandated an intolerance of low test scores and normalized severe approaches to expunging anything but high test score production. In this policy landscape Ms. Khoury's approach exemplified the fourth intervention strategy.

In her initial talk to the staff, she told the school that she believed in hard work, setting high standards, and holding people accountable to those standards. Even though Franklin High was never designated a struggling school, her words echoed the vague political speech that heralded intervention models, so one of the teachers asked her to clarify what she meant by higher standards.

"Oh, yes, of course. Let me be more specific. I think this school should be a baccalaureate school, a true international school, where students are working for the international baccalaureate diploma."

Most of the staff simply blinked at this statement. International baccalaureates are common in wealthy circles, where the children of diplomats earn an advanced high school diploma by studying theories of knowledge, volunteering outside of school in high-profile organizations, and passing intense exams graded by reviewers across the world. Perhaps some staff members were thinking of students like Lina, who spend most of their time outside of school hours providing crucial child care for their families and who have little chance of ever traveling or securing a fairly paid job, having more curriculum and tests to deal with. Here was a third red flag.

While no one would ever want to keep Lina from setting and achieving loftier goals, youth like Lina also need realistic support to help them manage the actual contexts of their lives. This practical help is the surest way of securing immediate needs of shelter, food, and clothing so that larger and higher goals are possible down the road. Without focusing on what is most pressing and achievable, setting high standards can be akin to setting kids up for failure, casting them as collateral in the pursuit of high scores and prestige for the school.

It did not take long for the change of leadership at this all-immigrant high school to show. I was at the school visiting in those first few weeks of the new school year, touching base with many of the teachers and students whom I had grown to know over the years. I was walking down the hallway with Carolina, one of these students, during a passing period between classes, catching up on the summer.

"Que te pasa en el verano? Porque usted parece tan refrescada!" Carolina was telling me that I must have slept all summer because I looked so refreshed.

"Claro que sí porque no tenía la muñeca charlando constamente en mi cabesa." I teased her back that I was rested because I hadn't had her chattering in my head.

"Miss, tengo una pregunta about the college . . ." Carolina started to ask me a question.

"Shhhhhhh!!! No Spanish!" we heard from behind us.

Ms. Khoury was behind us with a purposeful but taut smile on her face, wagging her finger to communicate to us that English was the only language spoken in the school. We fell silent, and as we continued walking, I thought about all that I wanted to say about the strengths of bilingualism and the xenophobia that fuels English Only mandates. Research literature has proven that being bilingual is cognitively far more enriching than being monolingual and that synthetically eliminating the natural use of the first language is not the best way to nurture bilingualism (Brisk, 2006; Crawford, 2004). Debates about allowing people to speak their native language are born of an unfounded fear that they won't ultimately learn English, and perhaps of an even deeper fear that with the increasing Latino population in the United States, one day English may not be the single national language of the country (Macedo, 2000).

Over the years, I have taught, interviewed, and known many native-born Americans who have expressed such concerns, and these fears and views are part of what has fueled initiatives like the one in Massachusetts in 2002, which outlawed bilingual education in public schools, an initiative backed by a conservative special interest group, English for the Children, and Mitt Romney, who was then campaigning for governor of Massachusetts. This context is also part of what motivates all educators in international schools to help their students reach proficient levels of fluency in academic English. The simple fact is that these kids need that proficiency to have any hope of mainstream achievement in American society. While it is not close to a complete education, it is necessary. However, the best way to nurture this fluency is not the complete denial of their home language, which is too often the proposed solution. Part of Franklin's success was the fact that its staff was mostly bilingual and could understand better what was missing from the students' explanations of concepts to each other in class or after school, and reteach these missing pieces in English. In essence, by using multiple languages, teachers could determine if a student's struggle with some content was due to the content itself, an issue of translation, or an issue of expression. Without this ability to access what students understood in their home languages, discerning what students need pedagogically is much more opaque. But more fundamentally, by having multiple bilingual teachers who spoke a number of languages, the students were also in regular contact with role models who communicated strength in multiple knowledges, not assimilative and reductive reactions to diversity.

Although these thoughts were racing through my mind after Ms. Khoury had admonished Carolina, to utter any protest in Carolina's company would have been openly defying Ms. Khoury in front of her students. Although an adult and the building leader, she was still the newcomer to this school who perhaps simply (I hoped) needed to learn more about immigrant youth and their needs. Around the corner, Carolina and I finished our conversation, in Spanish, and made a plan to go over Carolina's college application essay. I took that opportunity to confirm Carolina's instinct that there was absolutely nothing wrong with using her native language when she could, particularly outside of the English-only classroom context.

"I know, Miss, I think she just doesn't get it, you know? But it's OK, I know," Carolina assured me.

Later that day, one of the students pulled me aside and asked me if I had seen their planners for this year. I hadn't, but I was happy to see that the students all had planners with a page for each day, with space to keep track of their classes, and their assignments. It seemed like a good idea to me.

"No, Miss, you have to look here," Miguel pointed to the bottom of the page, which had six lines and above the lines, it said, Bathroom Passport.

"Miss, we have to have a teacher sign the passport if we want to go to the bathroom." He started laughing as I cringed. "Now we can be undocumented in two ways, not just one."

As I continued to spend time in the school over the next few weeks, it was simply unmistakable how the tenor and atmosphere of the school changed. The school's sole priorities quickly became students' class attendance and students' success in the state-mandated achievement tests. All staff members were to work singularly toward those two goals. While these are logical goals for a school, schools are far more complicated places than sites of test preparation. Schools are made up of people who spend all day together building relationships with each other. If the context is healthy, it's easier to have positive relationships that bolster learning. If it's not so healthy, this starts to show, with relationships fraying first at the edges around classroom spaces and then within the classrooms. This, then, impacts deeply the potential for any learning to occur (Rose, 1990). One of the reasons why Elvis worked so hard to succeed in biology is that he trusted and felt cared about by his teacher.

I had an opportunity to sit down and discuss some of my work at the school with Ms. Khoury. She listened carefully as I described the support mechanisms that we had been able to provide for undocumented students and the equally successful internship project where each of the seniors worked in an area business to expand his or her knowledge and interaction with professionals in the area. She took notes and listened, and then asked me one question.

"The work you've done sounds very interesting. This internship project is something. Can you tell me how that impacted their test scores or the dropout rate? Those are my two top priorities as the principal. We have to affect both of those." Now it was my turn to blink a few times.

"Well, the internship project was more about getting the students out of the comfort zone of the school, to put them in contact with professionals, while we could still provide support to help them understand the culture of American businesses," I explained further.

"Yes, but the dropout rate here is 35%. We have to attend to that first," Ms. Khoury explained further.

"Thirty-five percent? That doesn't sound right to me."

"Oh yes, it is 35%."

"Wait, are you measuring dropout rates based on who graduates in 4 years' time?" I asked. This is the federally mandated measure of dropout rates. Ms. Khoury confirmed that this was the measure she was using.

"Well, lots of ou- *[I started to say "our" and then adjusted my language]*, lots of the school's students need more than 4 years of high school work to achieve at levels comparable to native-born youth. Many of them stay here longer. Others return to their home countries before they graduate. Others transfer to other high schools if the counselors believe that they need a more mainstream environment."

"I understand that, but the measure is the measure." More blinking on my part. While the educational arena of high-stakes assessment focuses on measures like 4-year graduation rates, other numbers, such as student and staff absences, tell a different story.

The third week of school, a fight broke out at lunch, with some of the Dominican and Cape Verdean students getting into an all-out brawl that spilled out into the street in front of the school. While there were skirmishes here and there, the school had not yet seen a prolonged, physical, and violent fight in its history, and certainly not one that involved dozens of students and required police intervention. The incident jarred all of us, including the students. Perhaps it had simply been a matter of time, but few of us thought so. Those of us who had worked at Franklin under both Mr. Ojeda and Ms. Khoury felt the school morphing from feeling like a community to being a more individualized, and sadly far more typical, depersonalized large school culture. In these large comprehensive high schools, all of the problems that would normally be associated with depersonalized contexts crop up: fights, underachievement, and other distractions, all symptoms of alienation.

Under Ms. Khoury's leadership, the school became much more focused on being systematic in its organization and operation. The collection of achievement data had also been a top priority under Mr. Ojeda's leadership, but the key word here is systematic: Picture flow charts and diagrams. Teachers, counselors, and registrars now had more procedures and forms to track all the students in terms of academics and behavior. Mr. Perez, the school registrar, had always been tasked with organizing and maintaining the school's academic records, including individual students' schedules, but he had also been one of the strongest socioemotional supports for the students. In short order after Ms. Khoury took over, almost all of his time became occupied with completing and lodging these forms at the expense of his additional support for students.

Ms. Khoury was also adamant that students not be taken out of class for any reason, which affected Mr. Perez and all of the other student support personnel in the building. Instead of the counseling and person-to-person support that had formerly marked the school's culture, each student now had a 20-minute advisory period with an adult and 19 other students. Some teachers were initially relieved that students were no longer being called out of class to get help with college applications, to talk through family, legal, and safety issues, or to meet with associated professionals like me or paralegals. For teachers trying to cover content, interruptions like these are more than a nuisance; they infringe upon the classroom climate and culture. But while teachers are justified in wanting to protect their instructional time, students are not just students; they also need socioemotional support that isn't about osmosis or acute angles. This is one of the many complex tensions between valid competing interests that make up the infinitely challenging project of public education. As the school limited the ability of students to meet with adults outside of classroom instruction, the staff struggled to know the students as human beings with lives outside of test scores. For the adults whose passion was supporting these youth, the effects were immediate and demoralizing. They had gone from youth educators to reluctant bureaucrats. With fewer and less profound relationships with adult mentors, the students also acted out more, through fights, for example.

For turn-around principals, it's a good time to be an administrator in education. Superintendents and principals who take a hard line with staff and students, fire people, expunge schools of less desired students, and filter every activity through its potential impact on test scores are today's educational heroes. No doubt, a dogged focus on test scores will bring them up. Soviet Russia and apartheid South Africa, as well as many other authoritarian cultures, boasted well-oiled machines of education, where obedience and high standards were demanded and pursued relentlessly. To support those aims, these systems use honed procedures to weed out less desired children from the most intense and best rewarded learning streams (Chomsky, 2000; Spring, 2006). These are successful projects of test score production. They are not successful projects of democracy or, what I hold to be the purpose of education, of supporting all people to realize their highest human potential. A singular focus on test scores produces excellent students who achieve on their government's measures, but it also produces rather limited human beings and civilians, more equipped to perform on measures of studenting than, say, work collaboratively or think flexibly. Achievement on test scores may tell us something about their fleeting grasp of topics that someone somewhere has decided is important, but it tells us next to nothing about them as actual people.

The young immigrant students at Franklin went from being seen by the staff as human beings with complex life situations to being framed simply as contributors to, or more often detractors from, the school's collective report card. Unfortunately, the transformation of this school is typical of the current situation in education, in which school closings and takeovers by private corporations are commonplace (Fabricant & Fine, 2012). Without a doubt, public schooling has a long history of marginalizing some students while privileging others. The No Child Left Behind analysis of test scores simply confirmed what educators, parents, and children have known for a long time: For racially minoritized and poor children, schools are locations of social reproduction, where poor resources reproduce patterns of inequality in society (e.g., Anyon, 1989; MacLeod, 2009; Oakes, 1986). To put it bluntly, public schools' track record of social reproduction is largely indefensible. However, through sweeping top-down legislation that maintains a narrow-minded gaze on flat indications of a school's success with few supports for improvement, we run the risk of squelching the remote hope of ameliorating this longstanding pattern of American schooling. In this latest era of high-stakes assessment, poor Black and Brown children, including immigrant youth, are far more likely to drop out of school, be expelled from school, or be encouraged to transfer if their scores are too low. This tends to happen first to English language learners (immigrant students) and students with special needs, as these populations are not helpful to a school's overall achievement report card.

Educators who focus solely on test scores ultimately distance themselves from their students, who might be working a full-time job under the table outside of school, caring for their younger cousins when they get home, or becoming depressed and anxious with worry of being swept up in a deportation raid. The fact is that all of these life, or "extracurricular," situations impact young people and their learning, and if we are truly interested in education as the development of human beings, there is no shortcut to learning this necessary knowledge. It's messier and often without easy answers, but it's all part of the work.

CHAPTER EIGHT

You Must Be This Tall to Ride

In the last few decades the presence of both documented and undocumented immigrants has provoked public scrutiny and outrage, causing some immigrants to be vilified and others to be victimized, often for reasons that seem as arbitrary as height requirements at amusement parks. In June 2010 a particularly newsworthy detainment made national headlines. Eric Balderas, a sophomore at Harvard University, was detained by immigration authorities when he tried to board a plane from San Antonio to Boston using his Harvard student card and identification from the Mexican Consulate. When authorities continued to ask him for another kind of identification and insisted they were just trying to help him board the plane, Balderas started to worry. Balderas was born in Mexico but came to the United States, undocumented, with his mother when he was 4 years old. According to Balderas, his mother left her abusive husband and crossed the United States–Mexico border with the help of a coyote, a paid escort who charges between three and five thousand dollars to guide migrants into the United States. The use of professional coyotes has more than doubled (from about 21% of border crossings to more than 50%) after September 11th and the militarization of the border. The cost of border smuggling rises and falls in relation to factors such as border surveillance, demand for work across the border, and the relative health of the migrants. The business of coyotaje is a cottage industry rather than a large smuggling ring, characterized by small-scale coyotes with social ties to migrants.

For migrants, the journey across the border often ends in detainment, injury, and even death.. Eric Balderas and his mother were two of the lucky ones. They settled in San Antonio, where Eric went to school, consistently excelling in his classes. As his particular interest in science grew, he developed the hope of becoming a cancer researcher. In a local San Antonio newspaper, Eric was profiled for his acceptance into Ivy League schools along with two other San Antonio graduates. The newspaper article was called, "Hard work pays off for students." Eric was, in many ways, a virtual poster child for the DREAM Act, the legislative bill that proposes to provide a pathway to citizenship for undocumented youth who were brought into the country as children by their parents. Because Eric appeared clean-cut, was fluent only in standard English, and was on a sure-fire road to professional success due to his Ivy League education, he served as a fitting role model for the Dream Act, which appeals to the public based on the innocence of children and what they can contribute as U.S. citizens. After the media frenzy around his detainment, which included a Facebook page with over 5,500 members, U.S. Senator Richard Durbin championed Eric's case. When he was granted a work permit that would allow him to stay in the country, his former history teacher said, "It's like somebody up there understands the situation and that he's really a great person and the kind of people we want here in this country" (Sacchetti, 2010).

While individual cases sometimes garner media attention, these play out on a larger landscape of politicized differences between immigration policy, public relations, and stark statistics of visas, detention centers, and deportations. The record-breaking rates of deportation under the Obama administration have been met with some outcry. Subsequently, a formal policy edict in 2011 ruled that only migrants who were deemed to be serious criminal offenders would be pursued by ICE and that the agency would use a case-by-case basis to decide when to deport. While this policy was met with applause from liberal and Latino communities, in reality deportations remained widespread and were not limited to migrants with serious criminal records. In Eric Balderas' case, a large social network response brought awareness of the case to public figures who then campaigned on his behalf. In other cases where deportations have been stopped, it has likewise often been through a public outcry of this fashion (Preston, 2011). President Obama's election year announcement of promised leniency in deportation for immigrant youth is another act in this political field.

About the same time that Eric's situation was being covered in media outlets, Jean, an undocumented 21-year-old from Port-au-Prince, Haiti, was taking a community college class in Boston at international student rates, working 25 hours a week as a security guard on the graveyard shift, and lying low on his way to and from school and work. Jean had come to the United States 5 years earlier on a tourist visa and had been awarded temporary protective status by the Immigration and Customs Enforcement office based on volatile living conditions in Port-au-Prince. Jean had immigrated shortly after President Jean-Bertrand Aristide's last presidency, which lasted from 2001–2004, ended in a coup d'état. After the upheaval, Port-au-Prince simultaneously collapsed and erupted in chaos. Nicole Lee, a former resident of Haiti and the executive director of TransAfrica Forum, an advocacy group based in Washington, D.C., described conditions in Haiti as follows: "When Aristide was removed, water projects stopped, education projects stopped, healthcare clinics shut down. It wasn't just about removing a leader, it was about destroying a real democracy" (Scherr, 2009).

Extreme poverty and political upheaval set the backdrop for kidnappings and violent battery, particularly against more vulnerable young populations. Students in uniforms who were on their way to and from schools became quick and easy targets, as education was expensive and the private school uniforms were markers of at least some money. In Jean's family, education was a priority, and outside of food, it was the only legitimate reason for saving and spending money. They did not have a TV or new clothes or anything remotely resembling an electronic gadget in their home, as all of the money that Jean's parents earned went to feed and educate the children. After the 2004 coup d'état, Jean's parents scrimped further to send Jean and his older sister to the United States to forge a new and safer life. Upon arrival, both Jean and his sister were awarded temporary protective status (TPS) by federal authorities, which in 2005 led to residency for his sister, as officials determined that that it was unsafe for her to return to Haiti. However, when Jean appeared before a judge in 2007 to revisit his TPS status, the judge ruled that it was safe for Jean to return to Haiti and revoked the TPS. Jean had no idea why.

Not much had changed in Port-au-Prince during those 3 years between Aristide's removal and Jean's court appearance. But with that judge's decision, Jean went from a hopeful immigrant who aspired to become a doctor, to figuring out how to live under the radar of the authorities. As Jean recalls it, the judge simply told him that there was no longer any reason for him to stay in the United States and that it was time for him to go back. In court appearances like this one, which are more informal than a court hearing, there are rarely any proceedings from the hearing itself, so it is difficult to know what evidence and reasoning the judge used to make a decision. The lack of records also makes it difficult for immigration attorneys to advocate for their clients.

At Franklin High School, Jean was known for his quick and wide smile. He was the young man who turned in a lost wallet full of cash, held doors open for others, and picked trash off the floor, even if no one was looking. He had a kind of internal compass for doing the right thing. Jean could probably have made a misanthrope forget that most people are much crummier. And because he was so obviously authentic, it was impossible to get annoyed at Jean for being such a good person; it's just who he is.

Mr. Ojeda, the principal, started calling him Johnny Gorgeous, putting his arm around him when he saw him in the hallways, clapping him on the back and exclaiming, "Hey, it's Johnny Gorgeous! That's what I call him, Johnny Gorgeous!" Jean would smile even bigger, if that were possible, and wait until the public proclamation was over so that he could continue making his way to class. Jean did well in high school, and, like Eric Balderas, particularly enjoyed the sciences, biology best of all.

After high school, Jean wanted to continue with schooling, even at the international student rates that he would need to pay as an undocumented high school graduate. He had hoped that something was going to change in his reality, even though at many times he said he felt like a criminal who doesn't know what crime he committed: "I just don't know, Ms. Patel. I can't go back. And then I don't know why that judge thought it's OK for me to go back. And now I'm here, working, studying, trying to be good and do the right things, you know? But I just feel like a criminal and I don't know what I did that was so wrong."

Although Eric Balderas' hard work as a student had temporarily paid off with a full-ride scholarship to Harvard, Jean's hard work did not translate into university opportunities, and this discrepancy registered with Jean.

"Miss, did you hear about that kid from Harvard who got arrested by the immigration?"

"Yeah, Jean, I read about it."

"What do you think? They should let him stay?"

"Well, yeah, I think he should be allowed to stay in this country and continue with the life he's made here. He's a smart young man, like you, and we would benefit from both you and him being here."

Jean looked at me. "He came here when he was just a little kid. Do you think that's why it's different for me? Because I came when I was older, but he was just a kid?"

Jean and I had similar conversations several times over the next few weeks, while the Eric Balderas story remained a top news item in Boston. At different points, Jean asked if the difference in their stories was because he didn't speak accentless English like Eric, who had grown up in the United States, or if it was because he "didn't look so White," like Balderas. All undocumented youth struggle to make sense of their fraught circumstances, whether they wonder if God is punishing them, if they have not worked hard enough, or if they are simply not good people. Some sit uncomfortably with media campaigns that proclaim their innocence as children who were brought into the country by their "illegal" parents. They watch as their classmates go to college visits, get their driver's licenses, apply for federal financial aid, and travel back and forth from their home countries to the United States.

When his father died of a heart attack after Jean had been here for a year, Jean mourned not only his father's passing but his inability to travel to Haiti for the funeral. As the only son, he wanted to support his mother and to simply be there. Having to make sense of the loss of his parent while carrying two kinds of guilt—guilt for not being there and guilt for being in the United States but not at Harvard—made deep cuts in Jean's broad and wide smile. Jean was, in essence, trying to live within a multiedged case of what psychologists term *survivor guilt*.

When Jean asked why he was denied residency, he was also asking, in a broader sense, how he and Eric Balderas stacked up against each other in the eyes of American society and maybe in his own eyes. Jean and Eric were both alike and different in dozens of ways. They were both immigrants from poor nations that have intertwined histories with the United States. It wasn't just freedom from an abusive husband but also knowledge of the United States as a possible haven that undoubtedly led Eric's mother to embark on a dangerous journey with her preschool-aged son. Similarly, it was not just their hope of a safer life for Jean and his sister but also their exposure to the United States through military and federal presence that led Jean's parents to save for years to buy plane tickets from Port-au-Prince to the United States, rather than another nation.

Eric and Jean both aspired to careers in health care. Through different extensions into American education, though, those aspirations have taken different forms. Eric, having immigrated when he was 4 and speaking English all his life, could pursue Advanced Placement courses in science in high school, likely connecting him to a wider array of options as he thought about and refined his aspirations. Jean immigrated when he was 16 and spoke French and Haitian Creole fluently, but he had to learn English quickly to pass his high school proficiency exam and graduate. As laudable as both of their achievements are, by high school graduation Eric and Jean had already had qualitatively different experiences with schooling, professional cultures, and achievement. As Eric was writing a stellar college application essay that, in his own opinion, surely secured his acceptance into Ivy League schools, Jean was studying sample standardized assessments on the weekends to better understand the format and typical phraseology found in the state-mandated tests.

No doubt Eric and Jean both received critical assistance from adults in their lives along their pathways. That same principal who laughed loudly as he called out to Johnny Gorgeous in the hallways also drove Jean to and from community college two times a week, years after Jean had graduated from high school. However, unlike Eric, Jean had never encountered scientists outside of school, so his scientific aspiration was to be a doctor, rather than a more specific avocation, like Balderas' goal of becoming a cancer researcher. Put another way, Jean's contact with science as a profession was nonexistent. Details like these become important in understanding how and why Balderas was able to write a substantively different college application essay and why a case like Balderas' more easily catches mainstream attention, largely through social media. The terms of their inclusion in American society are marked more by difference than similarity, due to language, culture, and legal differences in their backgrounds, not due to differences in caliber of character.

When Eric Balderas was getting ready to board that plane in June, he later recalled that he didn't think anything would happen, "because it hadn't before." In interviews following his detainment, Balderas pointed out that he only has known America and feels that he is an American, a common plea for sympathy among undocumented children brought into the country by their parents. In contrast, Jean has known, in depth and detail, a volatile life in Port-au-Prince. Although he does not feel that he is only an American, he certainly has a close relationship with American society. He grew up accustomed to seeing American military men in uniforms in his neighborhoods and on the Port-au-Prince news, and most of his time in America has been under the shadow of fearing other Americans in uniforms. This type of exposure to better resourced cultures, which immigration scholars Alejandro Portes and Min Zhou (1993) have called "premigration acculturation," can have both positive and negative effects on people. Studies of immigrant youth and youth living in border towns, such as El Paso, Texas, show that, among immigrants whose home culture was not preserved to provide a sustained protective factor, substance abuse and mental health problems were more prevalent (Marsiglia, Kulis, Wagstaff, Elek, & Dran, 2005). While research grows into how immigration affects individuals, we also need better and more information about how to best support communities.

The immigration stories of both Eric and Jean are closely tied to their parents' histories. Eric's mother brought him here, through a dangerous and expensive clandestine journey, for a better life. Jean's parents made the equally difficult choice to forgo their need to care for and dote on their children daily and send them hundreds of miles away. These histories are shaped by transnational contexts in which the United States' economic and political involvement in nations like Mexico and Haiti is directly related to the quality of individuals' living conditions. The histories of wealthier and poorer countries are laced with legacies of colonization and exploitation that shape contemporary contexts. Sometimes individuals are able to break out of these histories of colonization to access a more coveted place in society, like being a student at Harvard University, but more often these legacies echo all too neatly in their life trajectories.

Jean kept asking about the differences between himself and Eric Balderas to try to make sense of his location in society, to determine what factors made the difference between criminals and Ivy League students, and to perhaps make sense of his own culpability for being undocumented. The one difference that he asked about more than any other was his age at the time of his entry to the United States. It is possibly more soothing, as a pat reason sometimes is, to Jean and youth like him to know that in the eyes of American society and some policies immigrants under a certain age are considered innocent, and their parents are the legally culpable ones. Easy explanations like this draw upon problematic sets of beliefs. The DREAM Act is premised on the idea that immigrant youth who have been brought up in the United States should be granted scissors to cut through bureaucratic red tape and claim their deep desire to be American. Appealing to this mind-set, hopeful undocumented immigrant youth, or DREAMers as they are called and sometimes call themselves, have gone to great lengths to prove their patriotism. In December 2010 DREAMers across the country participated in a blood drive to demonstrate their patriotism and willingness to perform community service. With activities like this, undocumented immigrant youth "out" themselves as being in the country illegally and use that temporary platform to raise awareness to tell their stories and show their worthiness as potential U.S. citizens. At its most basic level the DREAM act still perpetuates a view of immigration where individuals are acting autonomously, either legally or illegally, and should be judged according to characteristics that they can individually contribute to the nation. Obscured is the fact that immigrants and native-born residents act within a larger set of internationally mediated forces of economics and politics, possibilities and limitations.

Jean is in the United States without legal documentation, and this country would only benefit from his continued presence here. However, his immigration story, like so many others, cannot be understood even superficially based on just the time line of his physical migration. It is a story that involves agriculture, market economies, military force, government takeovers, poverty, rebellion, and oppression. Particularly against that backdrop, the designation of age limitations for pathways to citizenship is at best arbitrary and at worst willfully ignorant.

CHAPTER NINE

The Devil You Know

For undocumented students, the days stretch long during their junior and senior years in high school. While every other student is going on college visits, meeting with the high school counselor to go over admission and financial aid applications, and enjoying conversations with each other about colleges and majors, undocumented students are mostly silent and invisible. Rough, and surely conservative, estimates number undocumented youth enrolled in U.S. public high schools at about 600,000. These young people are, as immigration scholar Roberto Gonzalez (2011) put it, "learning to be illegal" as much as they are learning academic content. Undocumented youth quickly learn to evade questions from strangers about their plans for themselves after high school. Avoiding or dodging questions altogether is preferable to quickly assessing how much trust to place in a new person.

These questions came up one day when I was with Lina at a gathering of educators in Boston. Lina was taking a college class with me and working as a teaching assistant (TA) along with Jocelys, a Dominican immigrant with authorized permanent residency. After attending a talk about education and the civil rights movement in Boston, we were milling around the cheese and crackers, and I introduced Jocelys and Lina to Brenda, a colleague and friend who is a professor of education at another private, even more exclusive university. I explained that Lina and Jocelys were high school seniors enrolled in my graduate class and were working as TAs. Through a small grant from my university, I was able to give assistantships to a few of the immigrant youth each semester, choosing those who had mastered the context of their high schools and needed to be challenged further in their thinking, reading, and writing. At the same time, these youths provided input from their experiences with language, culture, and immigration into my classes of mostly U.S.-born, monolingual, middle class, and White graduate students. The high school students worked with me to prepare and debrief the class sessions and were exposed to worlds outside of their homes, friends, and Franklin High School.

"Oh, well that's just great. What a wonderful opportunity," Brenda smiled at the explanation for Lina and Jocelys being part of this audience among teachers and professors.

The two girls nodded and smiled; they had grown a lot during this college course, and both had met the challenge of pushing themselves out of the academic comfort zone of their high school.

"So, tell me, what are your plans for yourselves after graduation?" Brenda asked. It was March at the time, and most seniors who were able to go to college had already made their decisions about where they were headed for the next academic year.

"Oh, I'm going to go to Bridgewater State College," Jocelys said.

"That's great; it's a good 4-year college," Brenda said to Jocelys and then turned to Lina, who knew the question was coming her way. "How about you?"

"Oh, well, I'm still deciding, but I think I'm going to take some classes at Roxbury Community College."

"What?!" said Brenda incredulously. Thinking she was helping to motivate a teen who needed direction, she added, "If you're taking a masters-level class with Leigh, then you can't be taking classes at community college. That's just like high school with older kids. You should go to a 4-year college."

Lina smiled politely as this was not a new thought for her. Yes, her preference was to attend a 4-year college, but it wasn't a matter of motivation or desire. She looked over to me.

"Lina has some good plans in place for herself," I said, although both Lina and I disagreed with that statement. Because I was an adult and colleague of Brenda's, I could add a tone of finality to this part of the conversation, tell Brenda I would catch up with her soon, and steer Lina away from this line of questioning.

After this conversation, I contacted Brenda by phone. Because I knew and trusted her, I divulged to her that Lina was undocumented and therefore could not access higher education. I left out the complications of Lina's child care responsibilities in her family. One thing at a time.

"What? Oh my God, I had no idea. Would you please pass along my sincere apologies to her? Shit, I feel like such an idiot."

Brenda was justifiably mortified, and we spent a few more minutes in this loop of the conversation with me explaining that I wanted her to understand Lina's situation because there are so many undocumented immigrant youth in our high schools.

"And they just can't go to college? What do you mean? Is it an admissions problem?" asked Brenda.

"They are admissible, but they cannot qualify for in-state tuition, so they must pay out-of-state or international student tuition rates; and because they are barred from federal financial aid, that makes it impossible for the vast majority," I explained, pausing to let the nest of cumulative borders settle in layer by layer. "Even at a community college, the out-of-state tuition rate means at least $1,000 per class."

"Well, there must be something we can do. What about scholarships?" Brenda asked, sure that even if it had to be on a case-by-case basis, this kind of injustice must be solvable. Scholarships, however, often required citizenship and the big ones were highly competitive and in many cases linked to whom you knew. Piecemeal scholarships might cover a class or the cost of books for one semester. It simply didn't add up to a viable possibility.

"OK, listen, I'm going to call my friend Kathy, who works in policy and accounting; she must know of some sources. We must be able to do something," Brenda insisted. I thanked her for any help she might be able to garner, but asked her to just keep in mind that college isn't an automatic possibility for many low-income immigrant youth, documented or not. She assured me that she got it. Brenda did send me an e-mail later with the name of an organization that provides free financial counseling for high school seniors applying to college. These counselors help students work through the Free Application for Federal Student Aid (FAFSA) paperwork. For parents and kids trying to make sense of college applications and forms for the first time in their family's memory, these services provide a lifeline that helps make college a reality. However, this organization does not work with undocumented students; their website advises students without papers to talk with their high school counselors. This is but one example of the myriad blocks that exist and intertwine to prevent undocumented migrants from accessing safe positions in society. Up close, a single obstacle like financial aid seems manageable, but taken together with other societal blocks, the comprehensive picture of intertwined marginalization becomes clearer.

For Brenda, that conversation around the crackers and cheese was a gaffe from which she learned more about the immigrant youth in her own field of expertise. For Lina, that conversation was another reminder that she needed to be constantly on the watch for questions that could yield dangerous information about her. Just like when she watched her peers leave calculus class for college visits with their high school counselor, Brenda's questions pushed at the sore spot that even though she was a good student, worked hard, and had professional aspirations, college was not an option for her. In hindsight, their freshmen and sophomore years, marked by the initial struggle to learn English and academic tasks like formulating persuasive essays, were infinitely preferable to students like Lina than the incessant college banter permeating and simultaneously excluding undocumented youth from fully being juniors and seniors. To be undocumented means maintaining isolation and secrecy as a protective blanket, albeit a flimsy one. Every query about identity, citizenship, or status puts these kids on alert. Some college applications have blanks for Social Security numbers, and even though citizenship or residency is not a legal requirement for admissions, those blank spaces are enough for many undocumented youth to simply put the application down to avoid scrutiny.

Undocumented youth, who, like most other low-income immigrant youth, carry such large family responsibilities, also carry the surreal burden of hiding the most basic facts of their existence from their peers and even their best friends. When we were talking about college around the cheese and crackers,

Jocelys might well have been as confused by Lina's answers as Brenda was. Although Jocelys and Lina were good friends and laughed together about their teachers, assignments, and friends, Jocelys did not know about Lina's documentation status. Maintaining secrets like these takes a toll on these students, contributing to the isolation, depression, and despondency that are common among undocumented immigrants.

Having witnessed the isolation and frustration that so many undocumented youth experience in their final years of high school, some of the high school administrators and I started a support group of sorts for undocumented seniors. We had seen enough of the undocumented students graduate from high school and then live in very small worlds in which they rarely ventured out of their apartments or workplaces. We had watched as some of our brightest students spent their days babysitting cousins and neighborhood kids or playing video games or watching TV for hours on end, not because they wanted to but because there was nothing else for them to do. They had no sanctioned pathway to work or study, the most common routes for youth past their secondary years. As adults in their lives, we knew who was undocumented largely because the students trusted us enough to tell us and we compared what we knew with each other. While this granted us some measure of knowledge across the student body, we also knew that these young people did not have much opportunity to learn from people in similar situations or air their worries with their peers.

Our idea was to gather the undocumented seniors together a few times during the year in order to create a safe space for them to voice their internalized frustrations and worries and plan for some steps after high school graduation. We invited a few of the well-known graduates from the past few years, all undocumented, to sit in on the meetings and share some of what had helped them to stay busy and engaged after high school ended. We scheduled the first meeting after school one Monday, spread the word one-by-one to the undocumented students, ordered some pizza, and waited. We had no idea how this gathering would go over. If anything, we didn't have high expectations that this group of students would enthusiastically burst out of their protective shells and welcome this opportunity to share their experiences and plan out loud about their limited choices. Cultural practices as well as reinforced learning about the need to stay quiet meant that, minimally, these youth would not have questions, stories, or comments practiced for such an opportunity. In fact, a few of the 15 or so students were reticent about participating in the group. But they did show up, and most shared how frustrated they were that they were just as smart as the other students who were going to college. Many had no idea what they would do with their time after high school ended.

At one table sat Eduardo and Wana, the Haitian young woman from Chapter 1 who married and then divorced a U.S. citizen. At the time of this meeting, Wana was still undocumented, had moved back in with her aunt, and was taking a community college class, inching along in her nursing program while paying international student tuition rates. We had invited Wana in particular to talk about how she had learned that staying busy, even if it meant taking just one college class at a time, was better for her mental health and spirit than having too much time on her hands to think. She said a few words to the whole group of 15 students and then sat at a table to catch up with her friend Eduardo. Wana motioned for me and Mr. Perez, the registrar who knew the students very well, to come over.

"Tell them what you told me," Wana said.

Eduardo looked at both of us. He had immigrated from Guatemala with his mother, crossing Mexico by foot and traversing the border with a coyote, whom they paid $5,000 each for the border crossing. Since their arrival in Boston 2 years earlier, Eduardo worked in restaurants usually for about 40 hours a week. He maintained excellent grades, somehow managed to eke out time to be the high school's soccer team captain, and was a gentleman, through and through. In fact, when some of his peers faltered in their behavior, his soccer coach would often point to Eduardo, telling them to watch how he acted on and off the field and follow suit.

"Go ahead, tell them," Wana nudged, "They might have an idea."

"The problem," Eduardo started, "is not that I don't want to go to college or anything like that. I want to go, very much. It's better for me. Even if it means paying the full tuition and having to work a lot of hours to pay for it. I'm not afraid of working hard," said this young man, who traveled an hour on public transportation to get to school each day, and then an hour and a half after school to get to his job as a cook at a restaurant. He usually got home at 1:30 in the morning after working an 8-hour shift in the restaurant, only to get up at 5 A.M. to do some homework before doing it all over again. We knew he was not afraid of hard work.

"The problem is my mother. She doesn't want me to go," he explained. "She just wants me to keep working and save money, in case anything happens."

Mr. Perez and I exchanged looks. Mr. Perez, a community organizer with years of experience working with youth, looked Eduardo in the eyes and tried to explain a bit more of what his mother might be feeling.

"You know, Eduardo, my father is a very simple and strong man. Muy fuerte, me entiende?"

Eduardo nodded that he understood.

"He's a hard-working man who has always used his hands to bring money home and put food on the table. So when I," Mr. Perez motioned to himself and lifted up the fabric on the shoulders of his professional-looking button-down shirt, "told my father that I wanted to go to college and become an educator, se acabó la conversación." The conversation was finished before it got started.

"But you know, Eduardo, it wasn't because he didn't love me or want good things for me. It was because working hard, and working hard in manual labor with his hands, was all my father knew. It felt safe to him, like security and stability. Sí?"

Eduardo again nodded that he understood but added, "Yes, Mister, I understand, but I try to talk with her about it. I don't know, she don't listen." We asked Eduardo if he thought it might help if one of us were to talk with his mother.

"Oh, if you can make her listen so I can go to school, I would really appreciate that. I really want to go, but I can't go if she is against it, you know?"

Mr. Perez and I talked for a few minutes after the meeting about how the whole gathering went and the next steps for the students, but we spent particular time discussing Eduardo's situation. Even with our collective knowledge of youth, immigrant families, and the pressures of living undocumented and working for low wages, we were still reminded of and humbled at how much we as educators had to continually learn about our students' lives. Like Brenda, who had learned about the barriers standing between undocumented youth and affordable higher education, we had been schooled on the ways that higher education can represent more risk than opportunity for low-income undocumented families.

For Eduardo's mother, every trip to college meant that Eduardo would be riding on the public transportation system and waiting at bus stops, often within sketchy neighborhoods, where fights broke out often, and police officers asking questions followed. It also meant filling out forms about residency, meeting still more new people who had questions. All of these public spaces and interactions could bring unwanted questions, unwelcome scrutiny from office workers, and perhaps even confrontations from authorities. All the while, the threat of deportation loomed heavily over their heads. They were well aware that since immigration has become such a contentious issue in the political landscape, deportations and raids have skyrocketed.

If they were deported back to Guatemala, Eduardo and his mother would need money, not community college credits. But given Eduardo's strong desire to attend college and the enormous potential we saw in him, Mr. Perez and I decided to try to convince his mother to let him attend college. We also decided that it would be better for me, another female and someone from a college but also familiar with Eduardo, to go and speak with her. I called her and arranged to go there one Saturday afternoon.

I sat on the couch in their apartment, sipping hot, sugary, thick coffee and nibbling on the dulce (sweets) that Eduardo's mother had served. We made some small talk about the early heat of this spring, what a good student Eduardo was, and how well he had done working with another instructor in my college department.

"Que buen hombre, su hijo—uno de los mejores (What a great son you have, a good man, one of the best)," I said to Margarita, Eduardo's mother.

"Sí, sí, es un buen hijo, siempre trabajando y siempre me ayuda con la casa tambien (Yes, a good son, always a hard worker, and helping me around the house, too)," she answered.

Margarita worked the second shift as an office cleaner, and like Eduardo, was paid under the table at about $7 per hour. We spoke a bit longer about cleaning offices, as I shared that I had done this work as a teenager while going to school. We laughed about the messes that professional people could make—fuera de sus proprias casas (messes they might not ever make in their own homes). After a few minutes, when we had grown more comfortable with each other, I remarked that Eduardo was going to graduate soon and that he wanted to take a few college classes at a time, while he continued to work.

"Que le parece, Señora?" I asked Margarita what she thought of Eduardo's wishes. Even as I was saying these words, I worried that I was about to present a case for college that would be more simplistic than the reality was.

"Bueno, para mi, sería mejor continuar trabajar, guardar dinero. El hace muy bien en el restaurante, les gusta mucho, y es mejor continuar allí." In her opinion, it would be better for Eduardo to continue working in the restaurant where they liked him and he was doing well. He had been given a raise of fifty cents an hour recently.

I concurred that Eduardo was doing well at the restaurant and added that this was similar to how much all of his teachers liked him and always wanted to recommend him for helping other students or leadership roles in classes. "Sí, sí, un buen tipo." She agreed again that Eduardo was indeed well liked and well regarded wherever he went.

I told Margarita that, in some ways, Eduardo reminded me of Nicolas, an immigrant from Haiti who had graduated from the high school 2 years ago. He had been a top student like Eduardo who, like Eduardo and his mother, didn't have documents. He continued to work in odd construction jobs after high school but only spent time with friends at work, and this lifestyle took a toll on him. After a few years, he wasn't as interested in the world around him; he became depressed, and found it difficult to motivate himself to get out of bed every morning.

"Se pasa, a veces, cuando una persona es muy intelligente como ese tipo, y como Eduardo, que de no continuar con aprendaje, es casi como si se le muriera algo muy profundo en la alma." I said gently that sometimes with very intelligent and perceptive people, like Nicolas and Eduardo, when they are not in nurturing, learning spaces, something deep inside dies. Margarita looked between her coffee cup and me. I reached out to clasp her hand.

"Y, además, entiendo muy bien que, con cada paso, hay un montón de riesgos. Entiendo, señora, pero no le gustaría que nada se pase con Eduardo.

Tengo mucha confianza en su capacidad para tenir su cabesa. Y si va al colegío, yo estaré para asegurar que todo va bien." I validated her fears about the mountain of risks found outside their apartment door, but also I reminded her that Eduardo was very savvy about being careful and always kept his head. She looked me in the eyes when I said that if he took a few college courses, I would be there to make sure everything would be all right. This was a promise that I could keep on some levels, like smoothing Eduardo's transitions into college and making sure that he was put in the correct classes. But I was powerless, as were they, in the face of the all-too-real threat of deportation. Saying that everything would be all right was the oversimplification that I had been foreseeing and dreading in the earlier moments of our conversation, but I did not know how to get around it. As teachers, counselors, and confidants, service professionals working with immigrant populations all too often find themselves trying to portray and facilitate a straightforward pathway in a society riddled with blocked opportunities, contradictions, and risks.

"Sí? Usted va a estar con el al colegio?"

Would I really be there in his college if he went? I assured her that I would go with him to register, make sure that his classes were the right ones, and check in with him every week. I also told her that I liked the community college where Eduardo would take two classes in the fall very much because the people there seemed like good people, and I felt comfortable with the thought of him being there. Although I didn't explicitly mention it to Eduardo's mother, the professionals at this community college, who worked with lots of immigrant students, knew more about undocumented students like Eduardo and their needs than many of the better known academics from more prestigious institutions. I had sat in the admissions office with some of the high school students and watched as admissions officers treaded lightly, seeming to sense from downcast eyes or hesitations if documentation was an issue. I also saw them then realistically reassure the students that they could still attend the college but that it was going to be more expensive.

Margarita squeezed my hand tighter, and we reached what seemed like an agreement that opened up a door to college for Eduardo. It was a completely rational fear of visibility and the unknown that made Margarita wary of college. College-educated parents want their children to go to college because it is good for their children, but also because it's what they know. For many upper-middle-class and upper-class parents, the option of taking a year off before college to tour the world sounds like a life-enriching opportunity for their children. For a working-class parent, it might sound more like a huge waste of money and irresponsible; it's all a matter of what you know. Similarly, Eduardo's desire to go to college without the hope of completing a diploma in anything close to 4 years made little sense to Margarita.

For undocumented immigrants, visibility is to be avoided at all costs. Sometimes this invisibility creates discomfort and frustration, when, for example, students are forced to sit silently in class while other students are off on college visits. Undocumented youth must make an uneasy peace with this invisibility, knowing that it's necessary. Better the devil you know than the one you don't. This is also why, when immigration reform like Obama's election year executive order is promised, undocumented migrants often react with a mixture of hope and caution, weighing the benefits and risks of revealing their documentation status and fearing that policy could once again turn against them with the next change in the political current.

For educators, college is a tricky question. It is almost in our blood to want all of our students to go college because we believe firmly that a college education will mean a better life for them, bringing with it better salaries, better lifestyles, and security. However, college credits and even a college degree far from guarantee smooth professional sailing in contemporary society, with all of its social and political complications of who enjoys success and who doesn't. And college comes with financial ties. With more students attending college, a decline in a market for middle-class professionals with college degrees, and a shrinking base of federal financial support, college debt has risen to never-before-seen levels, surpassing credit card debt (Dynarski, 2008). In 2011, college loan debts in the United States hovered at a trillion dollars.

For many low-income immigrant families, the long-term promise of upward social mobility after years of college is in direct competition with more immediate needs of survival and safety. This tension is not easy to resolve and all too often, parents like Margarita are labeled as uninvolved in their children's education. The solution is not to change Margarita or parents like her, to ask them to attend more parent-teacher conferences, since none of those meetings would change the naked facts of these families' situations. Professionals like Mr. Perez know from a combination of experience and interpersonal craft how to find out about the social contexts of their students, often because they have some cultural background in common. For most educators who come from more established and status-marked suburban backgrounds, their students' lives are unfamiliar to them. Brenda's lack of knowledge about immigrant students' limitations echoed back to me as I learned about the dynamics where college felt more threatening than poorly paid hourly labor. Being an educator means not just knowing about youth but also constantly learning about their contexts and the forces that shape their lives.

Professionals like Mr. Perez taught me volumes about how to best serve populations like undocumented youth, who largely are invisible in their school contexts. And what magic did he do? He saw these young human beings not just as students, but as sons, daughters, and workers, acknowledging all of the roles they performed. He interacted with them as human beings and got to know their worlds as best he could. He advocated for them based on his best appraisals of their needs, the world in which they live, and he continually learned about these contexts.

However, no educator can fully address the enormous and constantly changing complexity of the immigration laws and contexts that shape Eduardo and Margarita's lives. Our best hope and central responsibility is to provide advice from a more informed position about our students' lives, to be humble and reconsider our own stances of college for all—to act, in essence, in the role of supportive and constant learner instead of vocalizing the scripts our jobs provide for us.

CHAPTER TEN

Measures of Adulthood

Once Eduardo's mother gave the green light, her bendición, for him to go to college, Eduardo wasted no time. He enrolled in two classes, with the cost of one class being covered by a grant from his former high school principal. Eduardo somehow managed to balance long commutes between home, school, and work. And, no surprise to anyone, he did not drop any hours at work. He maintained his schedule of over 45 hours of work a week at the restaurant and studied diligently for his two community college classes, Freshman Seminar and Introduction to Computer Science. Eduardo planned to become a software or website designer. He wasn't sure which one, but he knew that he liked the design and engineering side of computer applications and interfaces. Like most of the young people in this book, Eduardo consistently dusted off his goals and continued to pursue them, step-by-step, even in the face of dismal prospects for actually completing a college degree or earning a livable wage. As I've heard so many undocumented immigrant youth say, "I have to hope that someday something is going to change."

One day something did change for Eduardo. His father came back into his life. Eduardo's father, Francisco, immigrated to the United States years before Eduardo and his mother and settled on the East Coast. He secured stable employment in a factory, remarried, and had two more children with his new wife, Graciela. When Eduardo and his mother arrived in the states, after crossing the border on foot, Eduardo's father was very clear that he wanted nothing to do with either of them. This did not come as a surprise to anyone; Francisco had not exactly been an involved husband and father when the family was together in Guatemala, and he explicitly and purposefully left Eduardo's mother behind when he came to the United States. However, now that Eduardo was within reach of a stable future in the United States, Francisco's rebuff of his family not only delivered the expected emotional blow but also sealed Eduardo's fate as an out-of-status immigrant; his father, as his only blood relative with citizenship, was the only one able to sponsor Eduardo's citizenship. Despite numerous appeals from Eduardo, his mother, and a few of the school staff that Francisco sponsor Eduardo for citizenship before his 21st birthday, he remained firm. So for 3 years Eduardo worked for miniscule wages in restaurants without any benefits or worker protection. Being a fast worker was what made him valuable to his employer, but if he were injured, he would be ineligible for workers' compensation and would likely lose his job if he missed any days.

Eduardo studied hard in high school and then in community college, maintaining fidelity to the idea that education is the gateway to a vibrant and productive life. He gained the respect of his teachers, his bosses, his classmates, and everyone else. And much like anyone who is spurned by the blood relatives who are supposed to be genetically predisposed to protect and care for them, Eduardo quietly wondered why his father had rejected him so emphatically, but he moved on daily the best he could.

When Eduardo was 20 and going to community college and working, his father called him out of the blue and asked him to get together. He invited Eduardo over for dinner with his new family. Eduardo went, perplexed and not a little suspicious, but broke bread with his father, his stepmother, and his two younger half-siblings. Over the course of that dinner, many meals to follow, and the tentative relationship that developed, Francisco told Eduardo that he wanted to sponsor him for permanent residency and eventually citizenship. Eduardo was stunned, but concluded that his stepmother, Graciela, had been instrumental in this 180-degree turn-around.

"Miss, I think it was her. I think she was telling him to be a good father to me. That I'm a good man, and that he should support me, do something for me," Eduardo explained one day when we met to work on his resume. Just the week before, he had gone to the immigration offices with his father for his interview for residency.

"That's amazing, Eduardo. I'm so happy for you, but I'm just so surprised."

"Yes, I know, Miss, I was too. But you know," he waved the fingers on his hand like a teeter-totter, the universal sign for so-so.

"Yeah? You don't trust it? Or him?"

"Oh, no Miss, before we went to the immigration to do the paperwork, I made him sign a contract. I wrote everything that he was promising to do for me, and I made him sign it."

"Wow, Eduardo. Are you sure you don't want to go into law?" We both laughed. "Pero en sério, que fue? You know that the signed paper doesn't mean much to the authorities, right?"

"Yes, Miss, I know, but I wanted him to know that he was making a promise to me and that he should keep it, I mean this time. And I think that he knows he has not been so good to me. So I just want to say to him to really do it now that he said he was going to, you know?"

Yeah, I definitely knew.

Francisco did follow through, and Eduardo was able to petition for permanent residency, getting in before his 21st birthday just under the wire. He was issued a green card, and was euphoric about it, stating on his Facebook account that it was the happiest day in his life. Anyone not very close to Eduardo posted responses to his happy status, asking him why, it wasn't yet his birthday. Had he won the lottery? If so, they wanted some of it, they teased. He replied back to every person, "lol"-ing and simply saying that it was a very special day for him, still careful not to abandon completely his well-worn blanket of secrecy. But on the whole, he was ecstatic about the changes ahead of him, sure that things would be easier now that he could relax some of the protective reflexes he had grown over the past 3 years of being undocumented.

He decided to transfer to a different community college that had a larger repertoire of computer science classes. In the summer, he went to visit the admissions and financial offices. Admission was no problem, and as the proud and now visibly more relaxed holder of a green card, Eduardo was admitted and enrolled as a resident of the state, allowing him access to the much more affordable in-state tuition rates of $126 per credit hour instead of $332 he paid as an international student. He wanted to enroll for a full load of 12 credits. He was positive that he could lower some of his hours and pursue school more intently but he did not have the $1,512 needed for tuition and fees, and that didn't include books. Next stop: financial aid. That was when I got a phone call.

"Miss, are you busy? Can I ask you some questions?"

"Sure, what's up?"

"I'm at the financial aid office, and they are telling me that I have to report my parents' income to apply for financial aid. Is that right?" Damn.

"Yes, Eduardo, I'm afraid it is correct. You can't apply for financial aid as an independent. You still count as a dependent of your parents, so they want tax information for both."

This presented more than a minor challenge and no small amount of confusion for Eduardo. Exhibit A: neither of his parents had been providing financial support for him in more than 7 years. Exhibit B: Eduardo had been paying a healthy portion, often a majority, of the household expenses for the house that he shared with his mother and some extended family members, all of whom, except for Eduardo now, were undocumented. Exhibit C: His mother had not been filing tax returns. Many undocumented immigrants do file taxes and, in fact they are encouraged by immigrant advocates to do so to show that they are potentially "good citizens." The Internal Revenue Service estimates that undocumented migrants paid about $50 billion in taxes between 1996 and 2003. In addition to those who use fake Social Security numbers, many immigrants register for Individual Taxpayer Identification Numbers and file annually. If Eduardo's mother had filed for such a number, she might have been able to supply income tax returns, but this did not seem like a good idea. She, like many immigrants, are understandably terrified of creating any kind of a paper trail that might trigger and expedite deportation, or perhaps worse, be detained for years without any contact with family near and far.

"What did you tell them about your mother?" I asked.

"I told them that she's back in Guatemala and I don't have tax returns from there."

"And?"

"They said they want some record of her income there in Guatemala and of my father's income here in the United States, and then I can apply for financial aid. Miss, there is no other way?"

For more than 3 years, Eduardo had been working feverishly to support himself, his mother, and his family. He had been doing this while learning English, completing his high school degree, and then going on to community college. He had made sense in his mind, and whatever peace he could, with a mercurial father who had in essence dropped him from his life and then picked him back up. He had comforted, counseled, and learned to sometimes shut off from his mother who was bitter about the lack of support from his father. Judging by the responsibilities he held, he sounded a lot like an adult to me. According to federal financial aid statutes, though, Eduardo could not apply for financial aid independent of his parents because he was not:

- At least 24 years old on the day he filed for financial aid
- Enrolled in a masters or doctoral degree program at the beginning of the school year
- Married on the day he filed his financial aid application
- A parent
- Responsible for his own dependents other than a spouse
- An orphan or a ward of the court
- Currently serving on active duty in the U.S. Armed Forces for purposes other than training
- A veteran of the U.S. Armed Forces
- A foster child above the age of 13
- An emancipated child as determined by a court judge
- Homeless or at risk of homelessness

All of the stipulations require a paper trail or visibility in societal institutions that simply is not found in the lives of immigrant youth. This list is an apt reflection of the pathways for inclusion in society that are available for youth who are not following a typical family story, but they implicitly are designed for U.S.–born youth. As such, intentionally or not, they create conditions of inclusion to one of the lifelines to greater income potential: affordable higher education.

Eduardo enrolled in one class, which he could afford to pay for completely, including the books, out of his savings. He was back to the snail's pace that he'd been at before the gilded green card arrived. He also started applying for different jobs. With his green card, though, he was no longer such a great deal for his boss. Although his boss liked Eduardo a great deal, he told him he could not afford to keep him employed, or actually legally employ him as the case was, and pay him benefits and overtime rates. In applying for entry-level above-board jobs, Eduardo had a new field of competition, namely native-born citizens and legal residents who had been working longer in the United States and had resumes and sanctioned experience. After some months, he was able to find a job in a restaurant in a busy tourist area, where he worked 3 days a week while pursuing his one class at a small private college.

Just as the official immigration rules deem some illegal immigrants more sympathetic by virtue of having been brought to the United States when they were children, the rules that divide adolescents from adults and dependent versus independent status are arbitrary. This policy, like most, operate from an implicit cultural model of what is typical—in this case, what is the typical transition from child to adult. Looking over the list of qualifications for being able to apply for financial aid as a dependent, it is clear that the system is based on the idea of a "normal" kid who is supported by his parents through college and only after that will be on his own and able to support himself. That narrative of youth makes sense only for some populations, particularly those in which the passage from birth through stages of childhood, adolescence, and young adulthood is financed and protected by parents. In contrast, many immigrant youth are expected to be one of the pillars of their families, providing financial and cultural anchors in a new country. This is even further amplified if they are undocumented. They work long hours to keep themselves and their families in shelter and out of food lines. They may also deal with their own emotional needs and issues, protecting the adults in their lives from their worry, anxiety, and despondency and carrying some of their family's emotional burden as well. But, until they reach the age of 24, they are not considered adults.

Undocumented youths learn to live in the United States largely through the experience of lacking documentation. Being documented comes to hold an almost promised land feel to it. This is why Rebecca so aptly called it having the "magic" numbers. But even when documentation is no longer an issue, other borders to success remain intact and new ones appear, governed by many intertwining factors that open and close opportunities. What Eduardo learned is that even when he thought he had overcome the most important obstacle to success, his path to a better life was still far from unfettered.

CHAPTER ELEVEN

Black Market, White Market

Without a doubt, newcomer immigrant youth are some of the most capable residents in the nation. They are often skilled beyond their years and manage more responsibilities than lots of adults. If green cards and passports were awarded based on merit, most of the young people in this book, and countless others, would be offered them swiftly and without reservation. Unfortunately, documentation is not a matter of merit, and neither is societal status. But these youths' frustrating situations and the details of their worries and responsibilities as immigrants are only part of the picture. To focus solely on them, to even take on their plight and campaign for access to higher education for undocumented youth, is just part of the issue. A tight focus on immigration policy for individuals alone obscures the fundamental contexts that have created large populations of vulnerable workers in many developed nations. These kids and their struggles are just one part of the larger picture, which is characterized by the boundaries that society creates between migrant and native status, outsiders and insiders, and oppressed and privileged.

While Eduardo was figuring out how to convince his mother to let him brave the public transportation gauntlet in order to attend college, or Lina was at home babysitting her nieces, people in other social settings and classes went about their activities. As a university teacher and researcher, I benefit from the same system that blocks access to college for the youth in this book. On most days when I spend time with these youth and their families, I then go directly to teach a class on the campus of an elite private school or to a social event with others who benefit from the same educational system that these kids are excluded from, in many ways even squashed beneath. From this vantage point between these two different worlds, it is unmistakable that the plight of these youths as well as the relative safety and security of others more fortunate, are intertwined in a system that is structured on differential access and inclusion in society. While it may seem that bucking a globalized economic and political system that relies on global human capital is not easily tackled on a day-to-day basis, there are moments every day when the politics of inclusion and power are available for interpretation and negotiation.

One Sunday I attended a summer barbeque at a friend's house. I arrived a bit late and found my place at the outdoor dining table, making myself comfortable and helping myself to the chicken satay and peanut sauce appetizer. Most of these folks were in the upper-middle class and White, having settled into this environ of Boston, formerly an immigrant neighborhood, steadily over the last 10 years. As with many other urban areas that have experienced gentrification, the influx of young urban professionals, mostly White, brought with it a higher cost of living, which priced lower income populations of color out of the neighborhood, forcing them to move away. The neighborhood is now marked by the delivery of stainless steel kitchen appliances to recently renovated condos, corner coffee shops selling $5 lattes, and bistro restaurants providing ethnic food experiences. This is the neighborhood I live in. Like most people of color, it is with some degree of uneasiness that I live in my gentrified neighborhood. I prefer organic produce and want to be able to buy it in my neighborhood but lament that this all too often means living where I don't see my cultural background reflected. It mirrors, all too neatly, the racial and socioeconomic divides that plague this country and for which Boston is notorious.

This particular evening I met two out-of-town guests who lived and raised their families in a conservative mid-sized town in the northwestern United States. These visitors, while not part of this progressive political scene, were reveling in the liberal space, stretching their underexercised Democratic vocal chords. As part of the usual polite small talk about our occupations, I explained that I teach at a college and do research, which sounds far more professional and systematic than it usually feels in the daily moments. Since I spend the majority of my time with immigrant youth, I am considered "different" in these circles where almost everyone else works 9–5 in places that are temperature-controlled and cleaned by someone else, likely undocumented immigrants. So, I have "street cred." In contrast to reactions I received when I was a middle school teacher, which usually focused on aversion to adolescents, being a professor who researches immigrant youth is often met with more admiration and sometimes even outright appreciation for my "important work."

Still making small talk and getting acquainted, we looked for ways to connect our respective dots of experiences. After I shared what I do for a living and the kinds of classes I teach about education, culture, and society, one of the visitors commented upon how important she thought this work was and how vital it was to speak out against racism. She told a story about her daughter, who is half Puerto Rican and half Anglo (Mom's the Anglo), getting some flack on the bus ride home from a softball game.

"What are you, Mexican or something?" A boy had asked her on the bus, loudly, so that other kids would hear.

Most of the kids who did overhear probably either snickered or looked at her, actually wanting an answer that might explain her olive complexion in their all-White community.

"Well, my daughter just told him plain as day that she wasn't Mexican but if she was, she'd be proud of being Mexican! Nothing to be ashamed of," the mom recounted.

Her story was met with comments lauding the backbone of the 13-year-old daughter, and noting how important it was to have allies and supporters. It was the summer barbeque version of the golf clap. We moved on, and a few beats later in the conversation, this same Mom was entertaining the dinner gathering with tales of her larger-than-life elderly aunt, who had recently moved in with her, along with the aunt's pint-sized dog who had a predilection for either pee-ing on or chewing up the furniture.

"I'm telling you, can you even imagine moving into someone's house, bringing your untrained dog, and then just letting it mess all over?"

The laughter in response validated her opinion that no, this clearly was not to be done. Another dinner guest asked if the dog was so bad to require lots of cleaning. "I mean, like, do you have to get in carpet cleaners and new furniture?"

"Well, it's not sooo bad as all that, but I like things neat, you know? We, my husband and I, we did talk about getting some help for a while. In fact, we had things all set up to bring in this gal from Mexico, but that just kinda fell through, so I guess it's back to me and the yippy little thing."

While the dinner party laughed out loud about her description of the dog, I looked around for a reaction to this comment from the other, more seasoned, progressive Democrats around the table. Did it visibly register on anyone else's face that this woman had told inconsistently positioned back-to-back stories in-volving Mexicans? One was a case of mistaken national identity where her daughter was the hero for lauding Mexican national pride, followed by another where she was looking to pay a Mexican immigrant to handle some of the doggy pee and gnawed furniture leg cleaning that needed to be done. Her sto-ries progressed disturbingly from blunt-edged dismissal disguised as advocacy on a school bus to complicit exploitation of cheap migrant, and likely undocu-mented, labor. If this combination caused concern to register with others at the dinner party, I couldn't see it on anyone's face. Nor could they see it on mine. Just as the guests concurred that the aunt's behavior was unacceptable, it seemed that they agreed tacitly that the woman's stories, and the attitudes they exemplified, were acceptable, even desirable. The moment passed, and we went on to other topics of conversation.

As the conversation moved on, though, I was on edge. Truth be told, I had found both of the woman's stories disturbing. In the first, where the daughter had advocated for ethnic pride, it echoed the overly manicured and depersonal-ized advocacy of the type mocked by an episode of the television show *Seinfeld*. In the episode, the main character, who was assumed to be gay, denies it em-phatically but adds, "not that there's anything wrong with it," with his hands held up and fingers splayed to communicate a benign stance toward homosexuality. As with Radailyn and Yveline's exchange during the service trip to the Dominican Republic, there was the dynamic of one who enjoyed more power culturally, magnanimously, dictating inclusion and exclusion for the other.

How might the scene have gone differently if the daughter had challenged the question itself and refused to reveal her ethnic background, or if in the retelling of it, this was the point of the mother's story rather than how simply it had transpired? Telling a counterstory, or one that flips the frame on its side, is effective in pointing out the underlying assumptions that normalize inclusion and exclusion based on race (Delgado & Stefancic, 2012). For example, in spring 2011, in a deft political response to increased surveillance of immigrant populations suspected to be undocumented, many protestors took to wearing buttons proclaiming "I might be illegal." The slogan worked at a level of provocation because it indicted race-based suspicions of legal residency.

Granted, it takes dogged determination and dedication to confront the ways that society structures inequality, particularly if you benefit from that structure, but opportunities such as these to interrupt dominant stories are crucial for interrupting commonsensical views that it is legitimate for some to question others about their racial and ethnic heritage. Put another way, when our everyday stories perform into rules of inclusion based on race, ethnicity, and culture, we give credence to those criteria, and we lose the opportunity to confront the very mechanisms that sort insiders from outsiders.

In the second story, it wasn't so much the fact that this woman wanted to hire cheap immigrant labor for her house cleaning that I objected to. She's in widespread and even good company. For example, every one of the locals at the barbeque employed house cleaners who were, for the most part, Brazilian, undocumented female workers. Even those who were not undocumented were certainly not making a living wage. Headlines from newspapers regularly feature public officials, sometimes labor officials, snared in the photographer's flashbulb because they have been caught employing undocumented workers as their nannies, housekeepers, and landscapers. What really bothered me is that she made no apparent connection across the anti-immigrant sneer from the boys on the bus, the ease of a politically correct answer, and the perpetuation of a system that is defined by and relies on cheap human labor.

As I've spent more and more time with immigrant youth and their families and more advantaged native-born populations, I've come to understand how the personal narratives of both groups reflect different sides of the same larger systems of global economics, political treaties, and commercial interests. I've also become more and more dissatisfied with politically correct stances that feel good in the moment and conveniently but antithetically absolve individuals from reckoning with their place in the system. Living and working in a middle- and upper-middle-class environment in a Democratic state, I am bombarded daily with similar examples. Sitting at the dinner table, my heart felt a familiar indignation during the woman's second story, and my glance around the table was to see if anyone else was rankled. Because I could not see it, I said nothing. I am schooled well enough in the culture of this social class not to unthinkingly bring up a topic in which I am likely to be the only outlier. I was also conscious that, as the only person of color present, a curtain of awkwardness would quickly descend if I raised questions about race and how we decide to locate the limits of our advocacy. The dinner party might have devolved into something that felt more like a seminar on immigration, labor, and xenophobia. This would have been a topic not nearly as pleasant as where the recipe for the chicken satay came from, and in the American upper-middle class, pleasant prevails. My uneasy acquiescence to this code of pleasantry is part of what I've learned to do, as is true of most anyone who has crossed social class borders. As Gloria Anzaldúa (1999) captured in her classic treatise of hybridity, *Borderlands*, negotiating identity and voice at the interstices of competing social, political, and cultural forces is constant work. Anzaldúa's central point is not that only some people are border crossers and have hybrid identities. Rather, it is that because some experiences are normalized and therefore reflected more readily, those with marginalized identities have a hyperawareness of their hybridity, constantly monitoring themselves about how to navigate conversations, including even when to speak. It rarely is a simple location to be in and, given the same gathering on a different day, I might well have said something.

But as I let these statements go unchecked, as others at the dinner table also did, I became further complicit in perpetuating our places in this system and therefore the system itself. For me, it was that loss that lingered long after the meal was over. When we don't step up to the everyday challenges of educating ourselves and our young people for a more just society, we lose rich opportunities to interrupt complex patterns of inclusion, exclusion, and exploitation. For example, how might we seize a chance to disentangle why it's problematic for anyone to declare all nationalities as equal and worthy while her home reflects an ethnoracial labor division that fuels countless houses, offices, farms, and factories in developed nations? How might we help this daughter and others to understand and make sense of inequities, and not see them only as a matter of nationality or documentation status but as structured more comprehensively into a society premised on some having more than others?

Many immigrants find themselves with the short end of the stick not just with U.S. citizens but also with other immigrants. Rebecca, the salutatorian of her class whose pathways to sanctioned legal status in the United States disappeared when her mother was a no-show at a federal immigration hearing, did manage to secure a job at Dunkin Donuts. She landed this job using the Social Security number of another Dominican woman living in her apartment building. This woman, Bertha, had entered the United States with a green card and had recently given birth to a baby. Because she was not going to be using her

Social Security number for work outside of the home anytime soon, she offered Rebecca the use of her Social Security number and green card for a fee of
$200. Their agreement was that Rebecca could work using Bertha's documents
until Bertha wanted or needed to return to paid work herself. This agreement
worked fine until April, when Rebecca knew that Bertha would be filing taxes
with the IRS and paying into the solvency of the nation's Social Security system. Rebecca is one of the estimated 10 million unauthorized immigrants in the
nation now providing the once-teetering Social Security system with a subsidy
of as much as $6 to7 billion a year (Porter, 2005). The Social Security Adminis-
tration houses this surplus of billions in payments in an "earnings surplus file."
Rebecca's contributions to this file surfaced as an issue for her.

She texted me one day early in April and told me she had some questions
for me, so we met up after school. "Miss, do you know if there's going to be a
refund, cuz the income is so low, and she has the baby. My auntie told me that
she's going to get money back. Is that right?"

"Well, yes, there will probably be a refund. Did you talk with Bertha about
who gets the refund?"

"Yeah, I went to her right away when my auntie told me. And you know
that I know como hacerlo con respecto. I didn't yell or anything like that. I just
asked her about the taxes and if she was gonna give me the refund money."
Rebecca didn't need to tell me that she had approached Bertha with respect.
Rebecca was nothing if not composed and collected.

"And?"

"Miss, she say no, that she needs that money for her baby, and that I already got paid by the Dunkin Donuts. But, you know what? I kept all my, what
do you call it after you cash the check?"

"Pay stubs."

"Yes, OK. The pay stubs. I kept them all. I made like 8,500 dollars, and I
paid 1,000 in taxes. There's gonna be money back from the government, and
I'm not going to get any of that." She looked at me, arms folded, a cloud on her
usually bright face.

"I'm sorry, Rebecca, and you know this, but there's not much you can do."

"I know!" Rebecca said, obviously frustrated. "I know, Miss. But do you
think it's right what she's doing? It's not right, is it? I mean I already paid her
$200 and I could pay someone else on the street. Probably even less."

"I don't think it's right, but it's not just Bertha, though, right?"

Rebecca nodded that she understood but added, "I know that I don't
have the magic numbers, and that's not fair cuz I'm a good person and want
to go to college." She paused, not having the usual smile and demeanor she
had when joking about the magic numbers, and her voice got quieter as she
continued, "but it's not right that not having the numbers also means I don't
get paid the same as everyone else. For doing the same thing. And everybody
like me, we can't do anything."

She unfolded and refolded her arms. As frustrated as Rebecca was in this moment, I'm relatively certain she was not thinking toward her own senior years, when the Social Security system is supposed to pay her back for investing in it.

Rebecca had spent quite a bit of time investigating how migrant economies function within immigrant and native-born populations. She had been part of a small reading group from the high school that discussed portions of Bread and Roses, Bruce Watson's (2006) detailed account of the 1912 migrant-fueled strike and class-based uprising against unfair and dangerous labor conditions in textile mills in Lawrence, Massachusetts. We read portions of the book to contrast the social contexts of immigration and immigrant labor then to current trends.

Watson details the ways in which Lawrence was truly a town of immigrants, where the waves of immigrants, regardless of nationality, followed distinct settlement patterns. The sequence usually followed this order: A group of immigrants would establish a church, form social clubs, open stores carrying goods from home, celebrate holidays specific to their nations of origin, create native language newspapers and radio shows, establish a political presence in the city's elected offices, and finally, accumulate personal property and status. In our after-school reading group and discussion, we contrasted this sequence of sanctioned, largely European-based immigrant settlement and the mill uprising with contemporary realities for undocumented immigrants and labor. The gradual establishment of cultural spaces, like the church and the bodegas selling empanadas and prepaid international calling cards were the same, but there the similarities ended. Undocumented workers, most of whom now hail from the Global South, cannot have a voice in politics or advocate for themselves against unfair private practices, and they need to save money rather than spend it on goods that might draw unwanted attention. While the mill workers in turn-of-the-century Lawrence protested and launched an uprising that left an indelible mark on class relations, labor practices, and unions in the United States, the picture is quite different for undocumented migrants today. For youths like Rebecca, their need to work positions them in undesirable and sometimes unsafe work situations that leave them vulnerable to exploitive labor practices. This exploitation also exists within the immigrant communities, as Rebecca's experience proves.

So, what has changed so drastically in the nation and world between the social contexts of a German immigrant in Lowell in 1910 and a Haitian immigrant in Boston in 2010? For one, we are now living in a fragmented globalized capitalist market, a phrase that geographer and environmental psychologist Cindi Katz (2004) contrasts to the overused and nebulous nomenclature of globalization. Katz explains that a fragmented globalized capitalist market readily connects those with high amounts of capital (corporation owners and shareholders), enabling expansion of their interests across nation-state borders. These connections facilitate the interests of corporations against low-wage workers who are kept in subordinate, vulnerable positions. Vulnerable workers and inhumane working conditions are necessary in this equation, as those living wages and security for workers would significantly cut into the profit margins of the international corporations.

The parts and labor that go into making stainless steel appliances are part and parcel of a fractured—in that it blocks mobility—globalized free market system in which supply and demand dictate wages, prices, and working conditions. The export of human resource labor, developed demand among nations for cheap goods and services, and multinational corporations that export and exploit labor needs offshore all exist because of a market mentality that pushes prices to the lowest point, where only cheap, desperate, and disenfranchised labor will work for the wages necessary to subsidize the costs of the lifestyles of the middle and upper classes. All the while, undocumented immigrants are villainized for everything from crime waves to bankrupting the social services of the nation even as they pay into the nation's Social Security system with no hope of claiming benefits. The boogeyman in this scenario is every kid in this book and countless other immigrants like them.

This nation and others like it (in many European nations, anti-immigrant backlash resembles patterns in the United States) rely on undocumented immigrants to supply a labor force that is willing to work in low-income jobs with unsafe conditions (Silverstein, 2005). The state-sanctioned citizens of these nations are calcified in their lifestyles, unwilling to stop consuming cheap goods and resources. When the U.S. economy collapsed in 2008 and the housing bubble burst, lacerating retirement accounts with its shrapnel, the government bailed businesses and banks out and urged everyone to keep investing in their 401ks. Most people did. When 70,000 gallons of oil spilled into the Gulf of Mexico from an offshore drilling explosion, a deadlocked Congress was busy standing off about an energy bill that called for expanded offshore drilling. Both of these examples illuminate the intractability that exists to preserve a standard of living in the United States that revolves around consumption practices and is heavily subsidized by the government. Cheap human labor is a necessary part of that project. It is also what creates the conditions for partial inclusion, to supply labor but not to be afforded basic civil rights like a living wage.

In the face of this steady and unwavering need for cheap, exploitable labor, smaller black markets in falsified government documents and coyotes to guide border crossings have surged. In the past 5 to 10 years, many former drug smugglers have switched from smuggling weed across the United States–Mexico border to transporting human beings because the profit margin is greater and the penalties upon capture are milder. Illegal immigration to the United States and other developed nations is another type of black market that is necessitated by sanctioned markets.

Just as crucial to a free market is advanced nations' involvement with poorer countries and its effects on the minds and souls of people in the Global South. Rebecca grew up seeing Dominican-born men returning to Baní regularly bearing gifts from the United States. Jean grew up seeing American soldiers throughout his native Port-au-Prince. This system of transnational interconnectedness, which depends on some having more and others having less, changed the course of these youths' lives before they had even seen U.S. soil. Rather than being a natural state of affairs, this system is perpetuated through conscious thought and action, in policies that inequitably structure economic and political relationships.

So, at that Sunday barbeque, as I declined a dessert of Bananas Foster, likely made with rum from Puerto Rico and bananas imported from Chile and sold for 39 cents per pound, I thought about the ways that little bits of knowledge and advocacy are dangerous things. Asserting that all nationalities should have pride is an easy way to feel like an advocate while avoiding responsibility for paying into a system of human labor that pushes immigrants from poverty and starvation in the Global South into precarious and vulnerable work in developed nations. To be sure, the daughter's staunch proclamation that she would be proud even if she were Mexican is preferable to a response of "eewwww, I'm not Mexican." However, when measured against the standard of challenging structured inequality, these two responses are not so different, as neither one speaks to the larger system. In fact, it's easier to enjoy the Bananas Foster if you've logged your advocacy for the day. Check.

This type of superficial advocacy also fuels countless fundraisers and service trips to places like Haiti. As I walked through the student commons on my campus one day a few years ago, I saw a large poster board next to a table covered with brownies, cookies, cakes, and candies. The table was being manned by three young women who were obviously undergrads at the college. The poster board read:

BAKE SALE FOR HAITI!!!!!

Haiti is the poorest country in the Western hemisphere.
The country has been plagued by four back-to-back storm systems.
The Haitian people were ALREADY in the midst of a food crisis
BEFORE the storms hit.
It is estimated that 60% of the food supply for them now has been
wiped out.
This is why we NEED your help.

Below the carefully hand-written statements and facts was a large color photograph of Haitians wading through a flooded street, many holding some

of their belongings on top of their heads tied up in cloth bundles. When someone buys a brownie, she gets her sugar fix and perhaps also assuages her need
to contribute to a "worthy cause." But that same person can go on blissfully
without understanding the interconnections that constitute the political and
economic relationship between the United States and Haiti. The circumstances
surrounding Haitian President Jean-Bertrand Aristide's removal were hotly con-
tested at the time and remain so. Aristide and many Caribbean-based supporters of democracy maintain that the coup was financed and facilitated by the
United States and France following Aristide's demand that France pay Haiti
over 21 billion U.S. dollars—what he claimed to be the equivalent in today's
money of the 90 million gold francs Haiti was forced to pay Paris after winning
its freedom from France (Miller, 2004). Conversely, the U.S. federal government claimed that Haiti was volatile and unsafe under Aristide's presidency and
his removal was necessary for national and international security.

The fundraiser bake sale for Haiti also provides little political education
of economic policies that have been guided by transnational commercial inter
ests and supported by international policies. For decades, the interests of the
United States and other nations have subsidized the formation of transnational
commercial interests that developed monocrops in many Third World nations.
These interests also positioned developed nations as the consumers of those
single crop products—for example, bananas from Chile, blueberries from Ar-
gentina, and artichokes from Peru. Peter Chapman's (2008) book *Bananas!* explores how the United Fruit Company, one multinational commercial interest,
shaped more of these economic and political realities than did formally sitting
governments. The development of these monocrops sets off a chain of largely
unanticipated reactions. In the case of Haiti, its inability to sell its smaller rice
crops in global marketplaces ruled by tariffs and subsidies combined with the
interests of sugar companies prompted the clearance of acres of hilly and mountain areas to produce more sugar cane in level fields. After the torrential rains
of the monsoon and hurricane seasons arrived, the damage was exponentially
worse to the level fields, which had replaced more varied terrain. The small
island nation had no way to sustain itself amidst the hurricanes that wrought
extensive damage on its land, which produced crops that were no longer viable
in a global marketplace governed by rules and prices set by developed nations.
In an unprecedented apology, United States President Bill Clinton admitted in
2010 that his administration's powerful persuasion of Haiti to drastically reduce
tariffs on U.S.–grown crops was made in the interests of farmers in Arkansas,
but crippled Haiti's own agricultural interests (Katz, 2010). Clinton apologized
after he had journeyed to Haiti following the 2010 earthquake, where he witnessed firsthand the devastation that was not solely "natural" in origin. The
U.S. soldiers who patrol the streets of Port-au-Prince elicit a mixture of relief,
resentment, and sometimes shame among the residents of this nation, the first

to lodge a Black-led revolution for independence. But this history is hidden on a poster that instead fronts images of poor Haitians in appeals for American undergraduates to help them.

Educator and activist Paulo Freire coined a term for this: *false generosity*. It's the idea that some acts of generosity are actually driven by concern about public perception and a desire to be seen as a politically correct, progressive person who says the right thing and contributes to the right causes. It means that driving an SUV is somehow easier to rationalize if I drive it to a fundraiser on occasion, and the harm done by buying cheap sugar is ameliorated if some of the sugar goes into bake-sale brownies. It also means that enjoying the significant privilege that comes with being White in this nation may be part of what is seeking to be offset by donating money to Afro-Caribbean residents of an island hundreds of miles away.

In the widespread and rampant development that is possible because of cheap labor, no one is disconnected from this system, no matter the political identity they assume. Rather, it is important that we all see how our places in the system of black and white markets are essential in perpetuating the system. By seeing these interconnections, these spaces where some are included in safety and prosperity and others are not, it becomes much easier to take the next step of agitating these practices of inclusion and exclusion. Without first recognizing positions in this system, though, we stand little chance of changing it.

The kids in these stories are my heart; I would take each one into my home given the opportunity. I would buy a thousand brownies if I thought that it did more help than harm in masking the larger rhythms of migration, national interests, and global competition. But these acts would do very little, on the grand scale, to interrogate and agitate a free market system that complacently accepts human casualties as the cost of cheap goods and services. As capable, skilled, and mature as each of these kids is, issuing them green cards only superficially addresses these much bigger issues. What about the other kids and adults who grew up, just like these kids, in U.S.-saturated environments of media, soldiers, and consumer products, and simply want more stable lives like the pictures in the magazines but didn't make their way onto the honor roll? What about the lifestyles of those of us in the United States who can afford cheap gasoline, clothing, and food, all subsidized by our government and facilitated through webs of cheap labor?

There's so much talk these days about how to fix immigration it should be written in capital letters: Our Broken Immigration System. Often on the list of suggested solutions are things like bigger, taller, and wider fences and programs for pathways to citizenship. But individualized pathways to citizenship worry me. If we develop a system of just cherry-picking some outsiders to have a little bit of one form of inclusion, we've done precious little to revamp a system built on delineating the boundary between insiders and outsiders. Just as there can be no black market without a white market, there can be no unauthorized immigrants unless there are also people, by the luck of their birthplace, who enjoy smoother roads to safety, status, and success. In times when every purchase and transaction in nations like the United States rests upon cheap, vulnerable labor, advocacy must start with seeing the global in everyday local decisions and conversations. It must start with understanding the real costs of these goods and services and hopefully, somewhere along the way, choosing to restitch lifestyles so that our investment in human beings rivals our investments in retirement accounts.

CHAPTER TWELVE

Rethinking Contact Zones

For decades, Boston has been notorious for being highly segregated along racial lines. Immigrant youths, the majority of whom work long hours outside of their high school days to earn money to support themselves and their families both here and in their home countries, are similar to most low-income immigrants of color in that they are in contact with more affluent populations, particularly more affluent White populations. They come into contact with them as the cleaners of their homes and office spaces, the cooks and waitstaff in the restaurants they frequent, the construction workers in their buildings, and as their child care providers. In other words, they are included in these social spaces in some tightly scripted ways, but excluded from a fuller expanse of interaction and benefit. This chapter explores the daily lives not just of immigrant youth but also of native-born youth to reimagine what might intentionally be changed about the way people from different social circles and backgrounds come into contact with each other.

Mary Louise Pratt (1991) defined *contact zones* as "the social spaces where cultures meet, clash, and grapple with each other, often in contexts of highly asymmetrical relations of power, such as colonialism, slavery, or their aftermaths as they are lived out in many parts of the world today" (p. 1). Pratt's concept has been taken up in many ways across locations. In the United States, her work is best known through the field of participatory action research (PAR), a form of research which privileges the everyday expertise that people hold about their experiences and brings together diverse groups to build collective, often less privileged, knowledge about society. PAR scholar Maria Elena Torre (2005) has extended Pratt's theories to frame research projects where very differently positioned youth and adults are able to experience and analyze power inequities together.

More fundamentally and immediately relative to immigrant and native-born populations outside of transformative projects like these, the most pressing insight of Pratt's conceptual model of contact zones lies not in the observation that these zones exist, but rather that they exist all too often very neatly. They exist without purposeful, engaged discourse across positions of inclusion and exclusion in society that might lift up, in order to affect difference, discord, power differentials, and conflicts.

As is the case for most other racially minoritized, low-income youth, many of the spaces where immigrant youths come into contact with cultures that are more privileged than their own (native-born, middle- to upper-class, of European descent, fluent in standard English) are marked by a depressingly neat reflection of the prevailing social order. In their respective societal roles, the rules of engagement are precise, so that little actual interaction and particularly off-script interaction occurs between better and worse positioned populations. Although we don't often talk about these rules of interaction, when brought to the surface, they offer a great deal of insight into the larger social order.

Jose has been working in American restaurants for 5 years, changing jobs fairly frequently due to new opportunities created by word-of-mouth recommendations of his excellent work skills. He has been undocumented since his entry into the United States from El Salvador, but has been able to hold consistent work as a cook and waiter in four different restaurants in Harvard Square, a much more affluent part of town than where he lives in Dorchester. He has, in fact, been promoted in several of these restaurants due in part to his ability to abide by the implicit rules of the contact zone.

"My bosses, they like me, because I work hard but also because I am polite and talk to the customers. I ask about their food; I smile, and I tell them to tell me or someone else if there is any problem with their 'experience.' My last boss, he taught me to say it like that because the customers like that word and then he also showed me when to go away because the customer doesn't want to talk for too long."

Even though he attended Franklin High School and lived in a neighborhood mostly populated by other Central American immigrants, Jose had regular exposure to contact zones, beginning before his physical journey from El Salvador to the United States. He had a considerable amount of premigration exposure to American culture through migrants from his town of El Salvador, who went back and forth between the two locations, often bringing back goods and products purchased in the United States as well as stories and tales of life there. Jose's premigration and postmigration work and education experiences present an overly ordered set of contact zones, ones where, as he articulated himself, the rules of engagement were clearly, although usually implicitly, delineated and followed. These rules serve to support the prevailing social order, or as Pratt (1991) refers to it, the preexisting trajectories of colonization, conquest, and domination that first brought these cultures into contact. When civilizations colonized other territories, their success invariably meant the obliteration and subsequent enslavement of the conquered peoples in service of the invaders' economic and social interests. What this means today is that when interactions between individuals of divergent positions in society obey rules that consistently position one to serve the other, this enacts domination and oppression that are centuries old.

In my work with both immigrant youths and college students, I have come to know young people who cross paths on a regular basis but live in extremely different situations. I offer these two contrastive examples to demonstrate the various ways in which different social locations, in an overlapping context zone, mean very different sets of obligations, opportunities, and challenges to people of different statuses.

Danilo and Chelsea, both 19 years old, live in the greater metropolitan area of Boston and come into contact with each on a regular basis at the taquería where Danilo works and Chelsea goes to buy food. Roja Taquería has four locations in the greater Boston area, all of them located close to avenues and strips where college students live. The taquería features made-to-order combinations of burritos, tacos, nachos, and side dishes like fried plantains. Particularly around lunch time, the line to place an order can be 20 or 30 people deep, but customers rarely wait more than 10 minutes, watching as the line cooks prep orders frenziedly.

One day, I was meeting with Danilo, one of the line cooks at the restaurant, on one of his breaks at the taquería to discuss his potential involvement with a student immigration advocacy group, when Chelsea came into the restaurant with two of her friends. When she recognized me from a talk that I had done on campus about race and education, she approached me to inquire further about the topic and how she could learn more. We had a brief conversation, and I introduced Chelsea and Danilo. As they acknowledged each other, it was clear that these two young people, almost exactly the same age and both graduates of American public high schools, came into regular contact with each other but knew little, not just about each other, but perhaps also about the ways that the circumstances of their lives had shaped their respective social locations. I asked them to keep daily logs of their activities, and it is those logs and interviews with them that offer insight into what trajectories are brought into contact zones.

Danilo is an immigrant from Guatemala. He and his mother crossed Mexico on foot with his grandmother when he was 16 years old. They did not have the money to hire a coyote so instead they used tips and assistance from friends on which routes to follow. They traveled at night and sought shelter during the day, each carrying a gallon of water, one can of food, and, if they could afford to buy it, a bottle of Gatorade. After 3 days of travel in the summer, Danilo's grandmother fell ill and died. When he told me this story, he had a rather flat effect, even when he explained that his grandmother had died of thirst on the journey.

"But I don't get thirsty too much," Danilo said shrugging his shoulders, with the very dry tone that I came to associate with him.

He had worked in the taquería for 2 years, going from a part-time dishwasher to a full-time cook due to his ability to handle a large volume of orders quickly and his strong English skills for dealing with customers. His days go something like this:

6 A.M.: Wake up and help his mother get his younger brother up and
    ready for school
7 A.M.: Take the bus and two trains to travel from his family's apartment
    in Dorchester to work in a more affluent part of Boston
9 A.M.: Arrive at work to begin the food prep for the day's production
7–8 P.M.: Leave work to begin journey home
9:30–10 P.M.: Arrive home

While explaining his schedule, Danilo provided more detail about how he
learned to take one bus and two trains to work instead of an alternate route that
would require fewer transfers. "The 45 [bus route] doesn't come on time and
sometimes doesn't even come. I make the mistake only the first time coming
here. Then I learned that I better take the 37 and spend more time on the two
trains. That way I'm not late."

Before he worked full-time at the taquería, Danilo had worked part-time
there and in other restaurants while he attended Lincoln High, a public school
with both immigrant and U.S.-born students. His counselor explained to me
that, as a student, Danilo stood out as being talented academically but also had
attendance problems. When his counselor and his teachers tried to encourage
Danilo to attend college or admonished him for missing school, he demurred
to their comments. He explained to me that he didn't want to tell them about
the time conflicts he had with his jobs or that paying for college at out-of-state
tuition rates was not a possibility because he needed to work to help his mother
support the household and send money back to Guatemala.

Chelsea is a sophomore from northern New Jersey and had wanted to attend this private liberal arts school since she was in high school. To inform her
decision, she participated in college visits to the campus two times before sub-
mitting her application. During those college visits, Chelsea met with professors
and admissions officers and toured the housing facilities on campus. "Everyone
was so friendly, and the campus just felt 'right' to me, you know? I know that
you have to weigh everything, but I also just trusted my gut to tell me what felt
like home, and this was it."

When she arrived to be a full-time student, she was confident that she had
made the right college choice, and her mother, who had also attended this college as an undergraduate, was proud to have this legacy in her family.

A typical day for Chelsea would go something like this:

8:30 or 9 A.M.: Wake up and go to the campus fitness facility to work out
    before the day's classes and studying
9–11 A.M.: Work out at the fitness center and shower/get ready back at
    dorm room

Noon–4 P.M.: Go to classes (Although Chelsea had an occasional evening
class, most of her classes were in the afternoon.)

"I focus better in the afternoon, so I structure my time and schedule to have
my classes then," Chelsea explained. "Dr. Rose [the associate dean for undergraduate students] was really great about helping us all to take an inventory of,
like, our study habits and then make our schedules around what works best for
us as students."

After her afternoon classes Chelsea, having already eaten at the campus
dining hall for lunch, would often choose to walk across the street from campus and get a few fish tacos or a bean burrito from Roja for her dinner. She
would almost always go with friends who were also finished with their classes
for the day, and they would socialize over their meal, often making plans
for studying and/or socializing in the evening or over the weekend. Chelsea
was popular with other students and involved in several campus-based student organizations, so it was rare for her to have an evening free of a social
commitment.

Through their words, it is easy to grasp how these students have a very
different interaction with their daily schedules and the simple act of being someplace at a designated time. Most simply put, Chelsea's story was characterized
by possibility and choice, whereas Danilo's was marked by limitations and obligations to meet basic daily needs. How they structured their time reveals a great
deal, but perhaps even more illuminating of how societal structures also impact
our thinking is how they talk about schedules, responsibilities, and choices. In
one finite detail that is particularly telling, Chelsea described how choosing her
university was a matter of what felt like "home," and the entire stance of regard-
ing place as a matter of choice is silent in Danilo's words.

For Danilo and Chelsea, their daily practices strongly reflect larger patterns
and structures of citizenship, race, gender, and class. This does not mean that
because Danilo is Latino and Chelsea is White that their roles in society are cast
in stone, but neither does it mean that these demographic details are irrelevant.
Race, class, and gender are interlocked in Chelsea and Danilo's lives, as they
are for everyone. Understanding how privilege is awarded in society is much
more accurately achieved by considering the contexts of individuals' lives. It
also sets a more informed stage for how we might pivot from an understanding
of structure to being active within these structures, perhaps even substantively
changing the structures. In the next section, I describe a deliberate attempt to
change the dynamics and flow of contact zones between immigrant youth and
native-born businesspeople through an internship project. A few caveats: This
example is not put forth as a model, example, or guide of any sort. It is, instead, a case in point that can be used to consider and assess how modifications
in structure can be made that might create outcomes that are not simply the
echoes of colonization bemoaned by Pratt.

Many young people have internships in their high school or college years. It is an entire realm of business unto itself. In Boston, there is, for example, a for-profit internship company whose only mission is to find and place young people in high-status internship positions. For this service, the internship locator charges upwards of four-digit fees. Most of the families and young people who are able to pay these fees are already located in a preferential place in society, and in this way, the internship further buttresses their social status.

Over the course of many years, as I listened to the youths and adults at Franklin High and worked with youths at other schools in Boston and in surrounding towns, one aspect of their lives became very clear: Without direct and critical intervention into their interactions with the dominant culture, immigrant youths would likely either stay in their service-industry roles or completely assimilate into a European American lifestyle, with at least some collateral damage to their home cultural identity. For several semesters I had students like Lina work with me in my college classes, which gave them sustained exposure to an upper-middle-class, English-speaking, mostly White environment. At first, when they worked in the class, many of the immigrant youths would be intimidated by the college students, but over prolonged interactions, supported by many conversations we had about success and status in society, they recognized that they had a unique set of experiences and skills that supplemented those of the college students. Other youths knew almost intuitively that, even though their social positions were almost diametrically opposed to those of the college students, this social positioning did not reflect innate ability. A conversation we had one day when I was walking on my college campus with a group of youth from Franklin High illustrates this.

"It's so green."

"And clean!" This was met with laughter and murmurs of agreement.

"Yeah, that's cuz you live in the 'hood and don't see any trees."

"What you talking about? Like you look like you're from here with your cheap-ass T-mobile phone! Sorry, Miss, but it's true."

They teased each other while laughing at how very obvious it was that they, with their baggy pants, large hoop earrings, and darker skin and hair, did not fit into this backdrop of mostly White upper-middle-class young adults who tended to sport a preppier style of clothing. Then the conversation turned to observations on the college students. "They [the college students] definitely look like they got a lot of money. Look at the clothes."

"Yeah, and they all holding the Starbucks cups. Mmm [head shaking]."

When this last comment was made, Davey, a young immigrant from Cameroon, looked around more intently, and posed a question: "Miss, do these students work?"

"Some of them do," I answered, "but most do not, not full-time."

"Mmhmmm," Davey said, his eyes still fixed on the students passing through the quad. "Do they speak a lot of languages?" Davey persisted.

This question was asked by a young man who had added conversational Spanish to his collection of language fluencies in rapid-fire fashion after moving to the United States. Spanish was the language of the hallways of Franklin, and after a few weeks' time, Davey had all of his Spanish-speaking peers rolling with laughter at his insertions of almost flawless Dominican Spanish into class sessions.

"No, Davey. Most are monolingual," I answered.

"Do they send money home to their families?" Davey asked.

By this time, his line of questioning was clear. The students watched the back-and-forth conversation as Davey followed his line of questioning, much like a lawyer, and I responded. Davey kept his gaze fixed on the college students, who were talking with each other on their way to and from class.

"I don't think so, Davey. Most don't work to support themselves, and most were born here, so I don't think they are sending money home."

"So, they don't work as hard as we do, do they?"

There was the zinger he had been building up. Davey turned to look at me in the face and asked more pointedly, "How come some people got it so good when they may be not as smart?"

This conversation was the starting point, the backbone, and the driving force behind the Critical Transitions Project, the internship, community research, and critical analysis project that I have been organizing with immigrant youth, high school educators, and business partners. Davey's questions point out the fallacy of the American Dream—or the American Hallucination, as one of my college classes renamed this ideology—that if you work hard, play by the rules, and are a good person, society will reward you (McNamee & Miller, 2004). Davey's questions also draw into focus how intelligence, which can be understood as one way of being a "good" person, is recognized and interrogates the premise that innate intelligence is the reason for visible societal achievement, such as being a full-time college student at an elite private school with few monetary obligations. The question brought to the surface essential questions about status and achievement and warranted a much more consistent engagement and consideration than we could do on that single afternoon. The critical internship project was designed to speak to these types of questions.

The goal of the critical internship project was not only to expose young immigrants to professional contexts but also to provide a space where critical conversations about power, status, and society would be required companions to the actual internship. The project has its roots in the work of Paulo Freire (1970), whose approach to emancipatory education with the poor in Brazil was to systematically investigate and articulate their worlds in order to be able to act on them instead of only being acted upon. His work has been the backbone of many critical consciousness projects, including this one.

In the internship project I acted as the lead facilitator, the supervisor of the students' experiences, and their mentor. In fact, all of the students related to me as a sort of teacher or counselor, an adult whom they had come to know through the school, but with whom they had also interacted outside the realm of academics. They knew that in my work as a professor, I analyzed society and education. Additionally, they came into contact with a few graduate students who worked to support the program by finding business partners, analyzing survey and interview data, and, sometimes directly interacted with the youth.

During the internship project, which lasted approximately 6 weeks, high school seniors reported to a professional worksite one day a week instead of going to school. Placements for the internships varied from for-profit business-es like real estate and Internet sales companies to government and nonprofit community-based organizations. After spending the morning at their internship sites, the students would come together as a group of no more than 10 students, and we would engage in critical conversations about work, status, and achieve-ment in society. These afternoon meetings came to be known as the breakdown time, in which we would share facts and stories from the internship sites and use the cognitive and linguistic tools of critical pedagogy (Freire, 1970) and critical race theory (Bell, 1992; Delgado & Stefancic, 2012) to interrogate indi-vidualistic explanations of how people attain status and how success and intel-ligence are assessed. Each week we also drew upon shared readings of texts by intellectuals such as James Baldwin, bell hooks, Edwidge Danticat, and the Blue Scholars, with the text selection initiated by me and then led by the youths, who shared texts that they found relevant to our core inquiries.

At their internship placements, the youths also researched the cultural, so-cial, and economic capital mix (Bourdieu, 1990) that led different workers to their career trajectories. Likewise, students interviewed and, in some cohorts, surveyed members of their families and communities about career pathways, status, success, and capital across migrations. Our overarching goal was to define the relationship between ability, intelligence, and capital with status in society. We questioned the viability of meritocracy. This component of the pro-gram, both in its focus and structure, marked the project as substantively differ-ent from more mainstream internship projects, whose goal is unproblematized interaction with professional culture—in other words, assimilation.

The deliberate attempt to create contact zones between low-income youths of color and native-born members of the dominant culture was initially predi-cated upon a belief and hope that, if it were done with a critical perspective, youth could learn about dominant cultural practices without sacrificing their home cultural identification, which tends to leave psychological and emotion-al scars. To that purpose, one of our key readings was bell hooks's (1989) es-say, "Keeping Close to Home," in which she details the dangers, complexities, and distinct losses that she has felt across the cultural spaces of the academy and home in her personal and professional journey as a daughter, public intellectual, and feminist.

However, within the cohorts themselves and in the breakdown sessions, there were several strata of contact zones, only one of which was the interaction of the youth with others in the context of their professional internships. Early in one cohort's internship project, students were sharing the results of interviews that they had conducted with professionals in their worksites and communities about career pathways and success. In the group discussion, Christina, a young woman from a politically connected family that enjoyed preferential economic and social status in the capital of the Dominican Republic, stated that she believed that her two interviews demonstrated that success in society is predicated upon meritocracy, adding that college was a requirement for societal safety and status. She offered the support of the interviews she had conducted with a small business owner and her father, both of whom had cited college as important for everyone.

"They both said that college was important, so you are successful if you go to college and then get a job."

Christina offered this opinion shortly after Allan had shared his interview with his mother, reporting that, since she had never gone to college, when she needed to find work outside of the home after the family's migration to the United States, she worked as a housecleaner in several of their more affluent Chinese acquaintances' homes. Allan had given his interview with his mother as an example of what he found to be successful: a deliberate humbling of oneself to support one's family.

Fernando, also from the D.R., pushed back on Christina, saying, "So that means that Allan's mother isn't successful?"

Christina looked at Allan and said, "No, I'm sorry, I didn't mean that about your mother. I'm just saying that everyone is telling us to go college and how important it is, and that's what they told me too, but that doesn't mean that it's true for your mother. I guess everyone can be successful however they want."

"Do you really think that or you just don't wanna diss his mother?" chimed in Magdana. "Like she doesn't want it bad enough?"

"Yeah, what about what happens when you go to college and then you don't know how to talk to your family anymore, like what we read," Fernando asked of the group, and of Christina, referencing hooks's essay. "People change when they go away. We're all *[motioning to everyone in the room]* already different from before [migration]. When I went back last year [to the D.R.] I felt out of place a little, kinda like I do here. Same thing is gonna happen if we go to college, and even that doesn't guarantee anything for sure."

We revisited this conversation several times as we discussed success, political correctness, solidarity to family and home, and the rather static images we have of trajectories of success as inextricably linked to college and financial achievement. Although not originally part of the project's design, to truly engage in the contact zone that was itself the breakdown session, we needed to name aloud the different cultural locations that came into contact those afternoon meetings. Some students, although they were all low-income in the United States, enjoyed much higher cultural, economic, and social statuses in their home countries.

In this and ensuing conversations, we explored how premigration mixtures of capital not only shaped migration journeys and lives in immigrants' host countries but also impacted realities long after physical migrations. These were difficult and messy conversations, as no one clean explanation could or should have prevailed for understanding social contexts. For some students, being U.S.-born automatically accorded more status in society. For others, race was part of the equation, but it could be hard to pinpoint exactly how sometimes. For still others, an individual's success in society could only be explained by his or her efforts; working hard and trusting that good things would happen was the most important value to have. Students' views covered many points in between these polarities.

To a person, though, we had all been influenced by meritocracy. And as we discussed the results of our surveys and interviews and their connection to sociological theories about agency within constricted structures, we were not always left with either a uniform or optimistic view of society.

"So, if I don't believe that you gotta work hard to be successful, what are you supposed to believe? That it doesn't matter what I do?"

Gerson's question stuck right into the heart of the dilemma; dispensing with a belief in meritocracy also means losing the most convenient and common rationale we have for why some people do better than others. He also worried that dismantling a belief in meritocracy would give some an excuse to put forth less effort in their lives.

"Yeah, but if you know better, you can't still say that stuff about one person deserves it and somebody else doesn't. And if you know better, you don't always blame yourself all the time. Maybe you even know how to be smart about other things, not just school," Melanie added.

Melanie echoed Freire's life work and mission that better understanding our lives, through systematic study of our worlds, opens up a different kind of possibility and agency than repeating patterns. Additionally, she was speaking about how we can be smart in all kinds of contexts, not just school, which we normally and singly associate with how people should perform intelligence.

In addition to creating deliberate spaces for these conversations, the internship project also featured strong feedback from the business partners. Most of the business partners were White, native-born Americans, who had little interaction with youth, particularly recently immigrated youth. In recalling his thoughts when he was first contacted and asked to host an internship student, Mark said, "I thought, 'Great. Do I really need this right now? Some kid showing up every week.' But I had a great time and looked forward to Alejandro coming each week." Mark's appraisal of Alejandro was echoed by all of the business partners, to a person. For both the immigrant youths and the adults in the project, the contact zone of the internship created an opportunity, which most embraced, to alter not just how they interacted with each other, but also what they thought of each other.

In more traditional educational curricula and programs, the goal is much more unidirectional: that young people learn decontextualized job skills. That type of goal is closely connected to the belief that with the right set of abilities and commitment, societal success is sure to follow. Our starting point was different, and was premised on a more nuanced view of society and inclusion, as well as a view toward the unique skills that immigrant youths possess. As immigrant youths who had crossed both physical and figurative borders, these young people were practiced observers. They all had extensive practice in observing their surroundings to note what is "normal" and what is not. Additionally, these young people had already had the life experience of seeing different ways that inclusion is afforded and withheld, in at least two national contexts. From that vantage point, they were, in many ways, more quickly and deeply able to name the conditions that equated with different types of inclusion.

The internship project was designed to provide this group of young people exposure to different social circles in order to research, understand, and change what counts as success and intelligence across different contexts. The project was also purposefully designed to provide lesser privileged people with the analytic and linguistic tools to name their realities, to not always reach toward another's definition of success but to determine for themselves what meaningful inclusion would look and sound like. In other words, it was designed to create a contact zone in which the goal was to change the scripts normally followed in those zones.

For much of this book I have discussed how American and international institutions, practices, and beliefs structure a system of full inclusion for some and partial inclusion for others, in exploitative fashion. Because most American policies and beliefs are represented by White people and institutions, it is easy see this book as an indictment of White culture and an adulation of immigrant culture. But this analysis of immigration is fundamentally about the politics of inclusion and how much those politics pervade social settings. Much like power itself, the fact that terms of inclusion exist is not necessarily evil or even bad. Rather, these terms should be viewed as a constant presence whenever a group coheres. In the ubiquitous process of defining ourselves, we also define who we are not. The more important observation and pursuant question is what values, and whose, are being used to decide those borders. Borders have never been, nor will they ever be, permanent. This applies to nation-state borders as well as the more subtle borders of adulthood and legality.

Neuroscientists urge us to vary our route home on occasion, to keep our brain circuits exercising beyond routines, which don't require much thinking. You don't need to move to a different home to change the pattern of what your brain knows as familiar. Similarly, our responsibility is to think about how to change the structures of work, school, family, religion, and other facets of our lives so that societal patterns might change for the better. Every day we live, work, talk, love, and play in societal structures. These moments are replete with opportunity to note and modify who is included and excluded in pursuit of a more equitable society. For those who resemble the young people in this book, who are held at bay by the riches of society, I hope that you minimally question on whose terms you seek inclusion. For those who are doing the naming of what is intelligent, desirable, and even legal, I hope that you pause to consider the vantage point that affords you this momentarily lucky position. The work of seeing our places in a society built on differential inclusion in order to change those conditions rests upon each of us.

Afterword

The stories in this book are told, in large measure, to illuminate the political struggle for inclusion and to detail how immigrant youths encounter many different kinds of borders in the course of their lives in the United States. However, the stories in this book are also stories of vibrant young men and women. I thought you might want to know where some of them are.

At the time of this writing, Wana is still working part-time in a health care facility, pursuing a nursing degree at a large public university, and living with her mother, whom she supports. Lina is working as the primary child care provider in her family and also holding down a part-time job as a hairdresser in a small town in Ohio. Matthias is a junior at the elite college where he was given a full-ride scholarship, majoring in political science. Rebecca is working as a nanny for a wealthy family in Boston. Elvis works full-time as a baggage handler at an airport and still spins regularly at neighborhood events. Jean, now technically a college senior, is taking one to two community college classes at a time and works full-time as a security officer in a warehouse. Eduardo is taking classes and working as an intern with an investment firm.

References

Adichie, C. (2009). *The danger of the single story*. [Video file]. Video posted to: http://www. ted.com/talks/chimamanda_adichie_the_danger_of_a_single_story.html

Ainsworth, M. (1989). Attachments beyond infancy. *American Psychology, 44*(4), 709–716.

Anyon, J. (1989). Social class and school knowledge. *Curriculum Inquiry, 11*(1), 3–42.

Alexander, M. (2010). *The new Jim Crow: Mass incarceration in the age of colorblindness*. New York: The New Press.

American Academy of Child & Adolescent Psychology (2011). *Facts for families*. Retrieved from http://www.aacap.org/cs/root/facts_for_families/facts_for_families

Anzaldúa, G. (1999). *Borderlands/La frontera: The new mestiza* (2nd ed.). San Francisco: Aunt Lute Books.

Bahrampour, T. (2010, May 7). Prince William immigration law remains controversial. *Washington Post*. Retrieved from http://www.washingtonpost.com/wp-dyn/content/ article/2010/05/06/AR2010050602382.html

Bell, D. (1992). *Faces at the bottom of the well: The permanence of racism*. New York: Basic Books.

Bonilla-Silva, E. (2003). *Racism without racists: Color-blind racism and the persistence of racial inequality in the United States*. Lanham, MD: Rowman & Littlefield.

Bourdieu, P. (1990). *The logic of practice*. Cambridge, UK: Polity Press.

Brisk, M. E. (2006). *Bilingual education: From compensatory to quality schooling*. Mahwah, NJ: Erlbaum.

Brooks. J. L. (Producer & Director). (2004). *Spanglish* [Motion picture]. USA: Columbia.

Brown v. Board of Education, 347 U.S. 483 (1954).

Bourdieu, P. (1990). *The logic of practice* (R. Nice, trans.). Stanford, CA: Stanford University Press.

California Newsreel. (2008). *Unnatural causes: Is inequality making us sick?* [DVD]. San Francisco: California Newsreel.

Chapman, P. (2008). *Bananas!: How the United Fruit Company shaped the world*. New York: Canongate.

Childtrendsdatabank (2011). *Immigrant children*. Retrieved from http://www. childtrendsdatabank.org/?q=node/333

Chinn, S. (2009). *Inventing modern adolescence: The children of immigrants in turn-of-the-century America*. New Brunswick, NJ: Rutgers University Press.

Chomsky, N. (2000). *Chomsky on miseducation*. Lanham, MD: Rowman & Littlefield.

Crawford, J. (2004). *Educating English learners: Language diversity in the classroom*. Los Angeles: Bilingual Educational Services.

Crawford-Brown, C., & Melrose, J. (2001). Parent-child relationships in Caribbean families. In N. Webb (Ed.), *Culturally diverse parent-child and family relationships: A guide for social workers and other practitioners* (pp. 107–130). Westport, CT: Ablex.

Decapua, A., & Marshall, H. W. (2010). Serving ELLs with limited or interrupted education: Intervention that works. *TESOL Journal, 1*(1), 49–70.

Delgado, R., & Stefancic, J. (2012). *Critical race theory: An introduction* (2nd ed.). New York: New York University Press.

Dodson, L. (2009). *The moral underground: How ordinary Americans subvert an unfair economy.* New York: The New Press.

Doka, K. J. (1989). *Disenfranchised grief: Recognizing hidden sorrow.* New York: Lexington Books.

Dynarski, S. (2008). Raising college enrollment. *Milken Institute Review, 10*(3), 37–45.

Fabricant, M., & Fine, M. (2012). *Charter schools and the corporate takeover of education: What's at stake?* New York: Teachers College Press.

Feliciano, C. (2006). *Unequal origins: Immigrant selection and the education of the second generation.* New York: LFB Scholarly Publishing.

Fernandes, D. (2007). *Targeted: Homeland security and the business of immigration.* New York: Seven Stories Press.

Freire, P. (1970). *Pedagogy of the oppressed.* New York: Continuum.

Gándara, P., & Contreras, F. (2009). *The Latino education crisis: The consequences of failed social policies.* Cambridge, MA: Harvard University Press.

Gonzalez, R. G. (2011). Learning to be illegal: Undocumented youth and shifting legal contexts in the transition to adulthood. *American Sociological Review, 76*(4), 602–619.

Harris-Perry, M. (2011). *Sister citizen: Shame, stereotypes and black women in America.* New Haven, CT: Yale University Press.

Hondagneu-Sotelo, P. (2007). *Domestica: Immigrant workers cleaning and caring in the shadows of affluence* (2nd ed.). Berkeley: University of California Press.

hooks, b. (1989). Keeping close to home: Class and education. *Talking back: Thinking feminist, thinking black* (pp. 73–83). Boston: South End Press.

Internationals Network for Public Schools (2011). *Our schools.* Retrieved from http://www.internationalsnps.org/our-schools/our-schools.html

Kanstroom, D. (2007). *Deportation nation: Outsiders in American history.* Cambridge, MA: Harvard University Press.

Katz, C. (2004). *Growing up global: Economic restructuring and children's everyday lives.* Minneapolis: University of Minnesota Press.

Katz, J. M. (2010, March 20). With cheap food imports, Haiti can't feed itself. *Current.com.* Retrieved from: http://current.com/1p5sc4c

Kumashiro, K. (2012). *Bad teacher! How blaming teachers distorts the bigger picture.* New York: Teachers College Press.

Lacayo, A. E. (2010). *The impact of section 287(g) of the Immigration and Nationality Act on the Latino community.* Washington, DC: National Council of La Raza.

Latta, R. E., & Goodman, L. A. (2005). The interplay of cultural context and service provision in intimate partner violence: The case of Haitian immigrant women. *Violence Against Women, 11*(11), 1441–1464.

Lareau, A. (2011). *Unequal childhood: Class, race, and family life* (2nd ed.). Berkeley: University of California Press.

Lau v. Nichols, 414 U. S. 563 (1974).

legaltimes (2009, May 26). *Transcript: Obama introduces Sotomayor.* Retrieved from: http://legaltimes.typepad.com/blt/2009/05/transcript-obama-introduces-sotomayor.html

Leonardo, Z. (2007). The war on schools: NCLB, nation creation, and the educational construction of whiteness. *Race, Ethnicity, and Education, 10*(3), 261–278.

Lesko, N. (2001). *Act your age: A cultural construction of adolescence.* New York: Heinemann.

Levitt, P. (2001). *Transnational villagers.* Los Angeles: University of California Press.

Lomawaima, K. T., & McCarty, T. L. (2006). *To remain an Indian: Lessons in democracy from a century of Native American education.* New York: Teachers College Press.

Macedo, D. (2000). The colonialism of the English only movement. *Educational Researcher, 29*(15), 15–24.

MacLeod, J. (2009). *Ain't no makin' it: Aspirations and attainment in a low-income neighborhood,* (3rd ed.), Boulder, CO: Westview Press.

Marsiglia, F. F., Kulis, S., Wagstaff, D., Elek, E., & Dran, D. (2005). Acculturation status and substance use prevention with Mexican and Mexican-American youth. *Journal of Social Work Practice in the Addictions, 5(1–2),* 85–111.

McLafferty, S., & Preston, V. (1992). Spatial mismatch and labor market segmentation for African-American and Latina women. *Economic Geography, 68,* 408–431.

McNamee, S., & Miller, R. K. (2004). *The meritocracy myth.* Lanham, MD: Rowman & Littlefield.

Miller, D. J. (2004, March 12). Aristide's call for reparations from France unlikely to die. *Inter Press Service.* Retrieved from http://ipsnews.net/news.asp?idnews=22828

Morrow, V., & Richards, M. (1996). The ethics of social research with children: An overview. *Children & Society, 10*(2), 90–105.

Napolitano, J. (2012, June 15). *Exercising prosecutorial discretion with respect to individuals who came to the United States as children.* Retrieved from http://www.dhs.gov/xlibrary/assets/s1-exercising-prosecutorial-discretion-individuals-who-came-to-us-as-children.pdf

Oakes, J. (1986). *Keeping track: How schools structure inequality.* New Haven, CT: Yale University Press.

Office of the Press Secretary, The White House (2012, June 15). *Remarks by the President on immigration.* Retrieved from http://www.whitehouse.gov/the-press-office/2012/06/15/remarks-president-immigration

Orellana, M. F. (2009). *Translating childhoods: Immigrant youth, language and culture.* New Brunswick, NJ: Rutgers University Press.

Orozco, M. (2006). *Understanding the remittance economy in Haiti.* (Paper commissioned by the World Bank.) Retrieved from the Inter-American Dialogue website: http://www.thedialogue.org/page.cfm?pageID=32&pubID=1016

Peart, N. K. (2011, December 17). Why is the NYPD after me? *New York Times.* Retrieved from http://www.nytimes.com/2011/12/18/opinion/sunday/young-black-and-frisked-by-the-nypd.html

Porter, D. (2005, April 5). Illegal immigrations are bolstering Social Security with billions. *New York Times.* Retrieved from http://www.nytimes.com/2005/04/05/business/05immigration.html

Portes, A., & Zhou, M. (1993). The new second generation: Segmented assimilation and its variants. *Annals of the American Academy of Political and Social Sciences, 530,* 74–96.

Pratt, M. L. (1991). Arts of the contact zone. *Profession, 91,* 33–40.

Preston, J. (2011, November 12). Deportations under new U.S. policy are inconsistent. *New York Times.* Retrieved from http://www.nytimes.com/2011/11/13/us/politics/president-obamas-policy-on-deportation-is-unevenly-applied.html

Pujolar, J. (2000). *Gender, heteroglossia and power: A sociolinguistic study of youth culture.* Berlin, Germany: Walter de Gruyter.

Rindenbro, U. (2011, October 7). The cost of sending money and the impact of technology. *Business News America.* Retrieved from http://www.thedialogue.org/page.cfm?pageID=32&pubID=2765

Romero, M. (2006). Racial profiling and immigrants: Rounding up the usual suspects. *Critical Sociology, 32*(2–3) 447–473.

Rose, M. (1990). *Lives on the boundary: A moving account of the struggles and achievements of America's educationally underprepared.* New York: Penguin Books.

Sacchetti, M. (2010, June 19). Harvard student won't face deportation: ICE defers on action on illegal resident's case. *Boston Globe. Retreived from* http://www.boston.com/news/local/massachusetts/articles/2010/06/19/harvard_student_wont_face_deportation/

Scherr, J. (2009, April 5). Haiti: Uncovering U.S. involvement in Aristide coup. *Axis of Logic.* Retrieved from http://axisoflogic.com/artman/publish/Article_55355.shtml

Schiller, R. (2007). *The economics of poverty and discrimination* (10th ed.). Upper Saddle River, NJ: Prentice Hall.

Sen, R. (2003). *Stir it up: Lessons in community organizing and advocacy.* San Francisco: Jossey-Bass.

Silverstein, P. A. (2005). Immigrant racialization and the new savage slot: Race, migration, and immigraiton in the new Europe. *Annual Review of Anthropology, 34,* 363–384.

Spring, J. (2006). *Wheels in the head: Educational philosophies of authority, freedom, and culture from Socrates to human rights.* Mahwah, NJ: Erlbaum.

Smith, L. T. (1999). *Decolonizing methodologies: Research and indigenous peoples.* New York: St. Martin's Press.

Suárez-Orosco, C., Bang, H. J., & Kim, H. Y. (2010). I felt like my heart was staying behind: Psychological implications of family separations and reunifications for immigrant youth. *Journal of Adolescent Research, 26*(2), 222–257.

Suárez-Orosco, C., Todorova, I. L. G., & Louie, J. (2002). Making up for lost time: The experience of separation and reunification among immigrant families. *Family Process, 41*(4), 625–644.

Thorne, B. (1993). *Gender play: Girls and boys in school.* New Brunswick, NJ: Rutgers University Press.

Tjaden, P., & Thoennes, N. (2000). *Full report of the prevalence, incidence, and consequences of violence against women: Findings from the national violence against women survey* (NCJ 183781). Retrieved from the National Institute of Justice and the Centers for Disease Control and Prevention website: https://www.ncjrs.gov/pdffiles1/nij/183781.pdf

Torre, M. E. (2005). The alchemy of integrated spaces: Youth participation in research collectives of difference. In L. Weis & M. Fine (Eds.), *Beyond silenced voices* (pp. 251–266). Albany: State University of New York Press.

Tuck, E. (2009). Suspending damages: A letter to communities. *Harvard Educational Review, 79*(3), 409–427.

Watson, B. (2006). *Bread and roses: Mills, migrants, and the struggle for the American dream.* New York: Penguin.

Wolfe, P. (1991). On being woken up: The dreamtime in anthropology and in Australian settler culture. *Comparative Studies in Society and History, 33*(2), 197–224.

Wyn, J. (2005). What is happening to "adolescence"? Growing up in changing times. In J. A. Vadeboncoeur & L. P. Stevens (Eds.), *Re/constructing "the adolescent": Sign, symbol and body* (pp. 25–48). New York: Peter Lang.

Index

About the Author

Lisa (Leigh) Patel is an associate professor of race, language, and education. Prior to working as a university educator, she was a secondary teacher, journalist, and policymaker. Throughout her career, she has worked with societally marginalized young people and activists, using participatory methods to both investigate and agitate differences in power and status. More of her work can be found at lisapatel.org.